The Farm

A family's relationship with its land

Billy Cate

ISBN: 978-1-09839-063-1

Dedicated to Nilla and Charlie Cate,
who together created the soul of THE FARM.

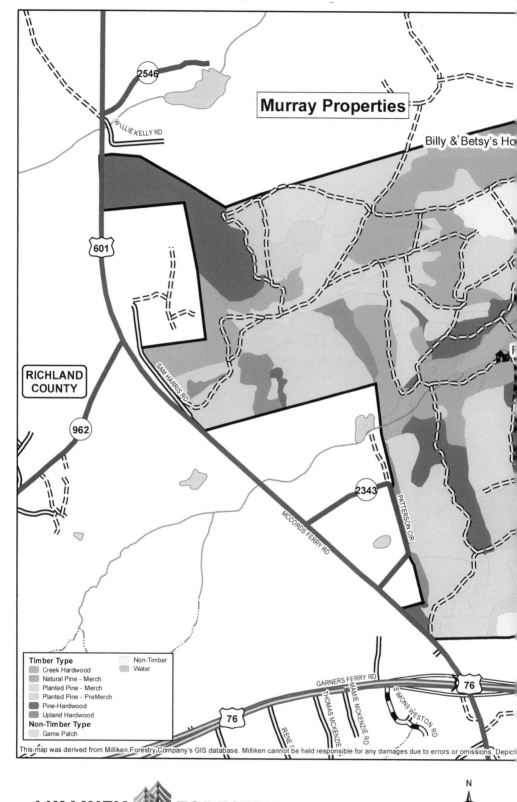

Murray Properties

RICHLAND COUNTY

Billy &' Betsy's Ho

Roads and labels:
2546
WILLIE KELLY RD
601
SAM HARRIS RD
962
2343
MCCORDS FERRY RD
PATTERSON CIR
GARNERS FERRY RD
76
THOMAS MCKENZIE RD
MAMIE MCKENZIE RD
S IMONS WESTON RD
IRENE
76

Legend:

Timber Type
- Creek Hardwood
- Natural Pine - Merch
- Planted Pine - Merch
- Planted Pine - PreMerch
- Pine-Hardwood
- Upland Hardwood

Non-Timber Type
- Game Patch
- Non-Timber
- Water

This map was derived from Milliken Forestry Company's GIS database. Milliken cannot be held responsible for any damages due to errors or omissions. Depic

MILLIKEN FORESTRY

Managing Assets Since 1949

N
W — E
S

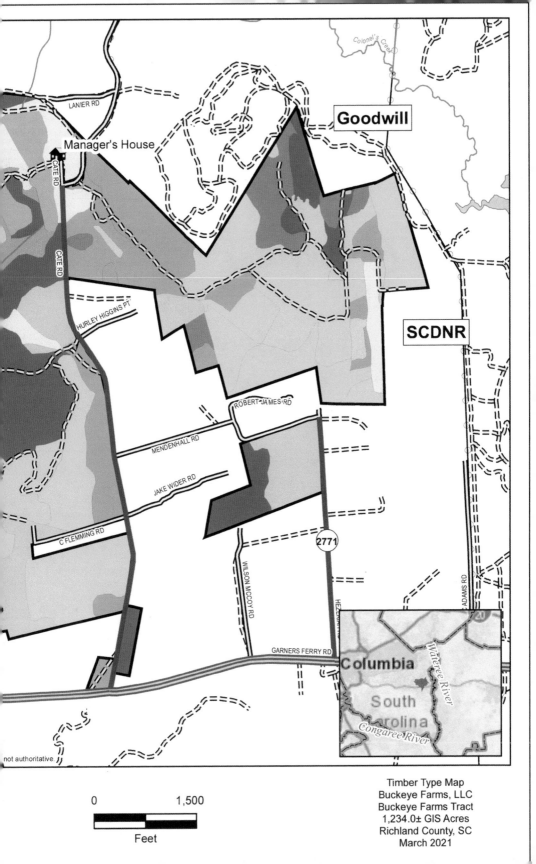

LANIER RD

Manager's House

CATE RD

CATE RD

HURLEY HIGGINS PT

MENDENHALL RD

JAKE WIDER RD

C FLEMMING RD

ROBERT JAMES RD

WILSON MCCOY RD

HEZZIE HILL

2771

GARNERS FERRY RD

ADAMS RD

Colonel's Creek

Goodwill

SCDNR

not authoritative.

Columbia

South Carolina

Wateree River

Congaree River

20

0   1,500

Feet

Timber Type Map
Buckeye Farms, LLC
Buckeye Farms Tract
1,234.0± GIS Acres
Richland County, SC
March 2021

TABLE OF CONTENTS

Foreword

Most of us South Carolina baby-boomers grew up in towns and cities or the thousands of suburbs that sprouted up across the state after World War II like dandelions in the front yard. But many of our parents came from farms, and in the 1950s many boomers still had a direct connection to South Carolina's rural roots. A holiday or summer vacation visit to Granddaddy's or Grandmother's farm was always one of the highlights of the year.

Unfortunately, that connection to the land became broken after our grandparents passed away. People had been leaving the countryside in droves since the end of World War I, and family farms were sold off or chopped up for real estate development.

A fortunate few, however, managed to hold onto their rural heritage. Such is the case for the Cate family. In this delightful book Billy Cate explains how his parents, Charlie and Nilla Cate, had the foresight to acquire farmland back when most others were giving theirs up. Buckeye Farms, named by Billy's mother for the beautiful dwarf buckeye plant that grows there, is a special place located in Lower Richland County in the heart of the COWASEE Basin.

Billy provides a long view of the sweeping changes that have affected farming and rural South Carolina for much of the twentieth century and beyond. Along the way we learn of a genuine western cattle drive that took place in Lower Richand in the 1920s; of valued farm managers and beloved dogs (including some that enjoyed watching television); learning to swim in a farm pond; the ins and outs of forest management; the devastating impacts of natural disasters, notably Hurricane Hugo and the Great Flood of 2015; the ebb and flow of various wildlife populations; Thanksgiving and Sunday dinner rituals, and finally, how a conservation easement came into being that protects the farm in perpetuity.

This book is not only about a farm but also about the family that goes with the farm. The two are inseparable, and for four generations of the Cate family, their farm has been a central theme in their lives. I think after reading this book you will understand why.

John Cely
February, 2021

Introduction

My father was born in 1901. My mother followed him eleven years later in 1912. They both lived long lives and saw many remarkable changes that shaped the Twentieth Century. It is now 2019, and I am 75 years old and have witnessed yet more incredible changes since their deaths in the 1990s.

This book is about our family's relationship with the land that makes up our family farm. I like to think that it is more than that however, as I try to describe the massive landscape changes that occurred from just after the American Civil War to the present time, not just on our land, but on farms across the Southeast. I will attempt to show how these changes impacted not just the people living on the land, but birds and wildlife of all descriptions, both native and non-native.

The history of our land is long. The Farm is roughly 1250 acres situated near the Wateree River in the heart of the COWASEE Basin in Lower Richland County, South Carolina in an area that was once flooded by sea water. Many millennia after the ocean receded, ancient Native American trails tracked through COWASEE up both the east and west banks of the Wateree River. When the first Europeans started showing up in the sixteenth century, these same trails were followed, and later when the first settlers arrived these trails became roads connecting Charleston and Camden. More about this when we get into the book, but sharp eyes can find evidence of these ancient cultures on our Farm as well as the neighboring countryside.

This book is intended to be a work of non-fiction, and I will try to credit sources wherever possible. I must confess however, that many of the sources are from family legend or from things I have been told over the course of my life by friends, family, and various mentors that are no longer available. That said, I plan to verify information wherever I can, but be aware that it is possible that some dates or facts could be misstated simply because I could not verify, and I remembered them wrong. Any such mistakes are unintentional, and I hope will not detract from what I am trying to report. The reason I am writing this book in the first place, is that over the years, I have frequently been told by friends or visitors as I've been showing them around The Farm, "Cate, you've got to write some of this stuff down." I have always responded, "Oh, I'm much too lazy!" I have more time now than I once had, and I have come to realize that I probably have more collective institutional knowledge about our land than anyone now living, and if I don't record what I know, much of it will become simply lost.

I used many different books as reference material or to get ideas about how to set something up. Among those that I relied on most heavily were *The Santee* by Henry Savage and published in 1954, *Sand County Almanac* by Aldo Leopold in 1948, *COWASEE Basin by* John Cely in 2012, *Seed From Madagascar* by Duncan Clinch Heyward in 1937, and *Looking for Longleaf* by Lawrence Early in 2004. Also helpful was *Hill of Beans* by John Snyder published in 2005, and a *Cultural Resource Survey Of Goodwill Plantation* written by the Department of History, University of South Carolina (Katheryn Hurt Richardson, Editor) and commissioned by Goodwill Stock Company in 1985.

Prehistorical and Early Historical

Many millions of years ago, following the various ice ages, the oceans rose dramatically, and seawater covered most of what we call our coastal plain. This means everything from the Fall Line (Think from Augusta, Columbia, Camden, Fayetteville) to where the ocean is today. A new ice age would begin, and the water would recede again, only to rise again as it ended, and the ice melted.

About two million years ago, and when the sea receded to approximately the level we know today, the Wateree and Congaree Rivers meandered through the alluvial bottomlands that had been the ocean floor to eventually merge to form the mighty Santee River. The Santee continued on with its load of silt from the piedmont to dump what it had not deposited along the way into the Atlantic midway between present day Georgetown and Charleston.[1]

Once the water receded and the land mass stabilized, flora and fauna not unlike what we know today developed. Trees and leafy plants appeared, and all vegetation was becoming much more specialized, adapting themselves to more varied environments. The forest settled in, and the stage was set for man although it would be many millennia before making his first appearance.[2] The Paleo-Indian Period began about 9,000 B.C. and melded into the Early Archaic period which is believed to have begun sometime before 6,000 B.C. and lasted until around 2,000 B.C. Very little is known about these ancient nomads, other than that they were hunter gatherers. About the only evidence that they were here are small white stone arrowheads.[3]

The Mississippian period of Native American culture

began around 500 A.D. and lasted until around 1700 A.D.[4] when regular European contact began happening. This period saw the development of much more advanced society, and evidence of this is well documented within the COWASEE Basin. Mississippian peoples were more dependent on agriculture and became very adept at corn cultivation. They had a much higher level of social organization revolving around chiefdoms. They constructed large ceremonial earthen mounds and developed very decorative ceramics. They are also known for creating beautiful spearpoints and arrowheads, which can be found up and down the Wateree and Congaree River basins where hunting parties frequently roamed.

Several of these ceremonial mounds remain along the Wateree near Camden, South Carolina, where the Cofitachiqui Chiefdom was located. In 1540, Spanish explorer Hernando de Soto made contact and visited the chiefdom on his well-documented exploration of the Southeast in search of gold and other treasures. De Soto entered what is now Richland County crossing the Broad River just north of present-day Columbia, and his foraging army of conquistadors followed Indian trails south along approximately where Bluff Road is today. They followed this trail down the east bank of the Congaree to where the Congaree meets the Wateree River forming the Santee. They then turned north and traveled up the west bank of the Wateree on a trail that approximates US 601 today. The original trail runs through the western edge part of our farm. They continued on north on this trail until making contact with the Indians just south of present-day Camden at Cofitachiqui. This is thought to be the first significant contact with Native Americans by Europeans in South Carolina.[5]

By the middle of the 17th Century, the English began arriving in Carolina coastal regions and established permanent settlements at Georgetown, Charleston, and Beaufort. It was hard enough simply surviving in the early settlements, and for many decades very little was known about the "Backcountry" as it was known at the time. In 1700 an English explorer with a very inquisitive mind named John Lawson spent several months exploring the interior of South Carolina. He took very detailed notes during his journey which provide a wonderful description of the land before it was settled. He traveled by boat up the Santee River to about where US 52 now crosses the river and then proceeded upstream on foot until he came

to the junction of the Congaree and Wateree Rivers. He
continued onward up the east bank of the Wateree along
an Indian trail along what is now SC Hwy 261 (the eastern
boundary of the COWASEE Basin) until he encountered an
encampment of Congaree Indians in the vicinity of what is
now Stateburg in the High Hills of The Santee. The Indians
were quite hospitable, and Lawson spent several enjoyable days
with them.[6] He describes in his writings the magnificent view
across the COWASEE Basin to the high hills on the other side
of the Basin in what is now Richland County: *"There appearing
great ridges of Mountains, bearing from us W.N.W. One Alp with
a top like a Sugar-loaf, advanced its Head above all the rest very
considerably"* From where he describes his camp, he clearly is
looking across the Wateree River Basin to what we now know
as Cooks Mountain, and quite likely is providing the first
written description of the part of the COWASEE Basin that I
call home.

1. Henry Savage, *The Santee* 1954, 1.
2. Ibid.
3. Kathryn Richards, advisory editor, *Cultural Resource
   Survey of Goodwill Plantation* 1985, 1
4. Ibid, 2.
5. John Cely, *COWASSEE Basin* 2012, 5.
6. Ibid, 3.

Charles Jacob Cate, Jr.
1901-1990

Charlie Cate was born in Wilson, North Carolina May 11, 1901 to Charles Jacob Cate, Sr. and Florence Spinks Cate. Charlie had an older brother, Henry, and three younger sisters, Emily, Geraldine and Mary Lilly. The family moved to Columbia, South Carolina in 1907.

Charlie entered the first grade at McMaster School in downtown Columbia, and oddly enough his first-grade teacher was Miss Nilla Perry, a name that will keep popping up throughout this book.

Shortly after moving to Columbia Charlie's dad, my grandfather, became friends at church (First Presbyterian Church in Columbia) with Samuel Buchanan "Buck" McMaster, and this friendship would greatly impact Charlie for the next 40 years and have a lasting influence for the rest of his life. Mr. Buck was a local entrepreneur, owning S. B. McMaster Sporting Goods on Hampton Street. S. B. McMaster Sporting Goods was a kind of general mercantile store that placed a great emphasis on hunting and fishing gear. The store was an institution in Columbia for many years. Mr. Buck was a noted sportsman and outdoorsman, and in 1909 purchased Goodwill Plantation from the Clarke Family. Mrs. Clarke was the daughter of P. T. Barnum of Barnum and Bailey Circus fame. In an earlier time Goodwill had been owned by several notable early South Carolina families such as Huger and Heyward. The property is located on the Wateree River in eastern Richland County about 25 miles from Columbia. As you will see, Buck McMaster and Goodwill will have a profound impact on young Charlie Cate, Jr.

At the time Charlie met him, Mr. Buck was still an "old "bachelor, being roughly 40 years old. He had access to great supplies of the latest hunting and fishing gear, and he owned a fabulous plantation that was a sportsman's paradise. Although cars were a rarity in that day, Mr. Buck always had one. Even with a car, the 25-mile trip from Columbia to Goodwill over very poor roads was a big deal. When he made his regular trips to Goodwill to check on things, he got in the habit of taking several boys from

Charlie with wild turkey killed in 1916 at Goodwill age 15

the church along to keep him company. Young Charlie Cate was invariably one of the chosen ones.

In the early days of the Twentieth Century Goodwill was a working "20 horse" farm meaning they were cultivating approximately 1500 acres using roughly 20 horses (or mules) and lots of farm hands to make that happen. On these jaunts to Goodwill, while Mr. Buck spent time with his foreman, the boys (many times it was just Charlie) fished and swam in the mill pond. In the fall and winter Buck introduced the boys to hunting. There were turkeys, and lots of Bobwhite Quail, and a few deer, but endless things for curious young minds to do. Young Charlie killed his first wild turkey at Goodwill in 1916 (age 15) with a Saur 20 gauge double barrel shotgun that was probably already 30 years old. This venerable shotgun is still in use in the Cate family today

Over time Charlie became very interested in the farming operation, and Buck rarely went to Goodwill without him.

They were often accompanied by another boy about Charlie's age, Walter Krell, or one or more of Mr. Buck's contemporaries, Dr. Fred Williams, or Clarence Asbill. When it became time for Charlie to go to college, he first enrolled in the University of South Carolina. While at Carolina, he continued to go to Goodwill at every opportunity, and became more and more interested and involved in the farming operation. Remember now, that in 1920 there were no tractors yet at Goodwill and still very difficult to get there. The more that he went, however, the more he realized that he wanted to go into agriculture for his profession. Once coming to this conclusion, Charlie decided to get a degree in agriculture. He ended up transferring and graduating from Clemson A & M College (Now Clemson University) in the Class of 1923.

Charlie and Mr. Buck circa 1920

After graduation, Mr. Buck hired Charlie to be the farm manager at Goodwill. This was a big job for such a young man. There were about a dozen families that lived on or around Goodwill who provided most of the labor for the farming operation. These families had deep roots at Goodwill. Most had been there for many generations and were descendants of slaves. Some had been slaves. Remember, that in those days farming was very labor intensive, and since there were no tractors yet at Goodwill, all tasks were performed by horsepower and manpower. For as long as he lived, Charlie remembered his days at Goodwill to be extremely satisfying and fulfilling. He was living in a virtual paradise, with all of the things he really liked to do at his fingertips. But make no mistake, life was hard. Besides the fact that he lived alone, there was no rural electricity provided at that time, which meant that there was no reliable plumbing. There was a water powered mill that served as a grist mill, saw mill and cotton gin. While Charlie lived at Goodwill, they figured out how to use the excess hydro capacity to develop a direct current (DC) generator and a ram powered pump to provide temporary and fairly unreliable electricity and water from the mill to the house. He had no car unless Mr. Buck was there. If he went somewhere he went on a horse or in a horse or mule drawn wagon. A trip to the town of Eastover and back would take a whole day.

Cotton was the main cash crop at Goodwill as it was on most farms in South Carolina. They also grew corn, potatoes and many vegetables to provide foodstuff for the families and the livestock. At some point while Charlie worked at Goodwill, they acquired their first tractor. It was a primitive affair with steel tires (I believe it was a John Deere). However, it was a hard time to be in agriculture. While the business world was booming during the Roaring 1920s, a nationwide agricultural depression was occurring. The Dust Bowl was raging across the prairies of the Mid-west and Southwest and farm failures were rampant. Cotton was the main cash crop in the Southeast and as more and more of it was being produced, the price started to drop. Most farmers were very unsophisticated in those days, and to counter falling prices, they simply planted more cotton making prices fall further yet. In about 1915 the boll weevil first appeared in cotton in South Carolina. Up until that time it was unknown. By the mid 1920s, boll weevils were causing wide-spread damage to cotton crops across the South. In those days, there was no known way to prevent them or destroy them once an infestation began. Needless to say, the boll weevil greatly added to the financial stress on cotton farmers everywhere as many complete crop failures began to be reported.

Always the entrepreneur, Buck learned of starving cattle herds in the West due to the terrible drought conditions, he and Charlie decided to purchase several rail cars of cattle at rock bottom prices and have them shipped by rail to Eastover seven miles away. From there they were driven by men on horses and mules to Goodwill where they were turned loose in the woods to forage on their own for whatever they could find. That cattle drive must have been a sight to see. While waiting for the cattle to arrive, they acquired lots of World War I surplus barbed wire and strung it around most of Goodwill's boundaries. The part of this history that I am not able to share is how this cattle venture turned out. I am not sure if I was ever told, but at any rate that information is lost. I am pretty sure that nobody got rich from it. Probably a good bit more beef eaten at Goodwill for a while though. I do know that the boundary between our farm and Goodwill is found by finding the 100-year-old WWI barbed wire that was strung around the boundary to keep the cows in. For the most part, the wire runs through the center of the trees that it was originally nailed to. An area on the eastern side of our Farm is known as the Wooden Gate. This is because when I was a boy there was an ancient wooden gate in that fence line hung between 2 hickory trees. The gate is long since disintegrated, but I could take you right to the old rusty hinges growing out of the old hickory tree.

Charlie did find time to do quite a bit of hunting and fishing however. As hard as farm life was in the 1920s, there were long periods of down time between seasons. Same as now, or before. That period of time was the heyday of the Bobwhite Quail or "birds" as they were always called. The birds were plentiful, and Charlie was passionate about hunting them. As long as I knew him, he always had at least one bird dog, even when the birds weren't so plentiful. In the wintertime, ducks were plentiful in the mill pond and the Wateree River and its surrounding swamp. There were some deer, but they were confined mostly to the river swamp at that time, and the only known way to hunt them was to drive them with hounds into a line of standers. There were some turkeys although their numbers appeared to be declining. One of Charlie's favorite duck hunting trips that he tried to do each winter, was to put a wooden fishing boat into the river at Basins Landing at the north edge of Goodwill, and paddle downstream to Ferguson , a logging village about 40 river miles downstream. Ferguson no longer exists as it was flooded when the Santee Cooper lakes were built in the 1930s. One of the men that lived and worked on Goodwill was T MacLemore. T always accompanied Charlie on these expeditions. He was not a duck hunter, but he was an excellent waterman and woodsman. T did most of the paddling and Charlie jump shot ducks out of the willow banks as they made their way downstream. It took most of 3 days to make the trip to Ferguson. They camped on the riverbank. Charlie and T remained friends long after Charlie left Goodwill. I can remember going as a boy to see T for visits with my father.

Sometime during the year 1930, Charlie concluded that it

was time for a change. Agriculture in the South was changing. The cotton economy was collapsing, and the country was dropping into the Great Depression. He left Goodwill with mixed emotions. He had loved his time there, but he and Buck realized that his future was probably brighter in a different type of career. As he left Goodwill, he made himself a promise that some way some day he was going to accumulate enough money to buy his own land close by in the same neighborhood.

While Charlie was grappling with trying to make a living farming, his older brother Henry was doing very well in the oil business in Texas. Henry had been pestering him for some time to come join him and get rich. That is exactly what he did after he left Goodwill, but it did not work out as planned. He was sent to a remote oil field near Midland, Texas. He was miserable. It was too hot or too cold, and the wind and dust blew most of the winter and spring. After a year of that he decided that he would rather be a poor farmer in South Carolina than a rich man in Texas any day! He was going home.

One of Charlie's first stops after getting back to Columbia was going to see Mr. Buck. He knew that he did not want to return to the farm at Goodwill. All of the issues that caused him to leave still existed, and had worsened if anything. The country was in a severe economic crisis as it dropped into the Great Depression, and agriculture had been wallowing in it for almost ten years. The one section of the economy that was thriving was the rapidly expanding automobile industry. Buck and Charlie put their heads together to try to figure out a way to hitch on to that expansionary growth. Cars and trucks needed tires, and lots of them. There was not yet a good distribution system for tire replacement at wholesale or retail levels. Buck used his influence to obtain the statewide distributorship for the Seiberling Tire and Rubber Company out of Akron, Ohio. Seiberling was a well known tire brand at that time that was later purchased by Firestone. At any rate, in 1932 the worst year of the Great Depression, Buck and Charlie formed McMaster and Cate Tire Company and began to sell tires at retail in Columbia and statewide at wholesale. They had guessed right, and soon found that there was indeed a great demand for tires for both cars and trucks. At first the tires were sold out of S. B. McMaster Sporting Goods. The tire business began to prosper and soon outgrew the sporting goods business and required more space. McMaster and Cate soon moved into a much larger space next door on the corner of Hampton and Sumter Streets. Charlie, at sometime prior to 1935, hired JW McLaurin to run the wholesale side of the business and he immediately became an important cog in the operation. When Mr. Buck died suddenly in 1939, Charlie bought some of the McMaster stock in the company, and McLaurin bought the rest of it, and they incorporated as Cate-McLaurin Co. Inc. The company prospered and evolved as times changed over the decades that followed, and it meant many things to many people, both customers and the many hundreds of employees that matriculated through the ranks over the years. I realize as I write this, that a whole book could be written just on Cate-McLaurin alone. That will have to be another project for another day. The whole point of this piece of background, is that from its beginnings in 1932, the Cate family hitched its family financial future to this thriving young business.

Charlie circa 1932

Nilla Perry Gunter
1912-1995

Nilla was born July 6, 1912 to Lueco Gunter and Laura Perry Gunter in Rock Hill, South Carolina. She had an older brother and sister, Lueco (Luke) and Margaret. My mother never liked her real name which was Leonilla Perry Gunter. She did like her nickname however, and always preferred to be called simply Nilla. In deference to that, when Betsy and I had our second child, a girl, and wanted to name her after my mother, we simply named her Nilla Perry Cate. Likewise, when our Nilla and her husband, Sam had their second daughter, they named her Nilla Perry Hesley.

My grandfather Gunter was a noted educator, having served as Superintendent of Schools in Beaufort, South Carolina, and then took a similar position in Rock Hill, South Carolina, where my mother, Nilla was born. The family then moved to Anderson, South Carolina where he served as Superintendent of Rural Schools in South Carolina. In 1918 he accepted a position as head of the English Department of Furman University, where he was highly respected and much loved. He became ill and died in 1922. He was 43. My mother, Nilla was 10.

After Lueco died, my grandmother, Laura, moved the family to Columbia and moved in with her sister, Nilla Perry. At that time they lived on Pickens Street across from the University of South Carolina. Laura got a job as a librarian at the University while Little Nilla's Aunt Nilla was an elementary school teacher at McMaster School 2 blocks north on Pickens Street.

Nilla's older sister Margaret became ill during a routine

Nilla second from right, with family on Pickens Street, circa 1922

medical procedure in 1926 and died shortly after. She was 19. This tragedy rocked her family. None of the remaining family members were ever able to discuss that event in a definitive way in all the years that I knew them.

Nilla went to the old Columbia High School, where she was voted prettiest in her senior class, and graduated in 1930. She then went to the University of South Carolina graduating in 1934. She was elected president of Tri Delta Sorority for her senior year. She always told me that honor gave her more confidence in herself than anything she had done up to that point in her life. I found that to be true when asked to lead my fraternity 32 years later.

Upon graduation, Nilla went to work for the Federal Land Bank. Sometime in 1934 or 1935 Nilla was introduced to Charlie Cate. My siblings and I are not certain as to the circumstances of this event, but our suspicions are that it was orchestrated by

Nilla circa 1930

her uncle Bill Perry (My namesake). Uncle Bill was a noted sportsman and also a contemporary of Mr. Buck and would have seen the matchmaking possibilities. At any rate, the electricity kicked in and a match was made! Charlie taught her to shoot and took her dove hunting, and she surprised herself to learn that she was a very proficient wing shot. He also taught her to drive, as women were just starting to regularly get behind the wheel.

Nilla as a bride in 1936

They were married in 1936. The electricity lasted and they were sweethearts for as long as I knew them, and they did almost everything together for as long as they lived. I heard almost no disagreement between them as a child or as an adult. If they ever disagreed, it was resolved quickly with no resentment. I think to all who knew them, it was a model relationship.

My brother Charlie was born in 1938 and my sister Betsy in 1940. I

Italy picture, circa 1980

followed in 1944. My earliest recollections are of the time at Goodwill and then the Farm, always the Farm. These early images are so imprinted into my childhood, they did much to shape the person I am today.

15

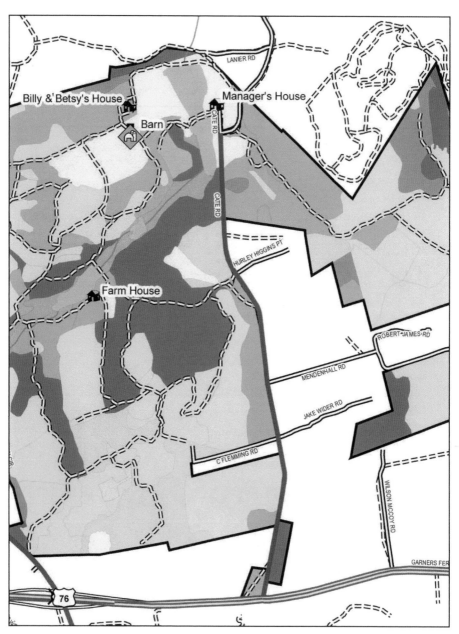

The original purchase of 140 acres where the farm house is located.

The Farm

The name of our farm is Buckeye Farms, and that is the name under which it does business. Our family, and most of our close friends simply call it The Farm. I am often asked where the name Buckeye came from. Well, there were some native red buckeye trees there (bushes really), and my mother liked them and planted some more, as well as some other varieties of buckeyes. She also liked the name – Buckeye. So, at some point in the early years, she decided to call the place Buckeye. As I said, we usually just referred to it as "The Farm". At the time when the Farm was incorporated as an LLC in the early 1980's as a more efficient means to do business and to transfer ownership when the time came, the name Buckeye Farm LLC was adopted, and the Farm started doing business as Buckeye Farms.

When Buck McMaster died in 1939, he left four of his closest friends unlimited, lifetime hunting and fishing privileges at Goodwill Plantation, no matter who owned the property. They were Dr. Fred Williams, Clarence Asbill, Walter Krell, and my father, Charlie Cate. All these men enjoyed the benefits of Goodwill for the rest of their lives. Charlie, being younger, probably received the most benefit from that most unusual bequeath.

At any rate, Charlie and Nilla would take their young family to Goodwill for long weekends or on vacation each year. Remember that when Charlie left Goodwill in 1930, he vowed that he would someday own his own land in the neighborhood. He and Nilla used their time at Goodwill to tour the area looking for land that might be available. In 1947 they struck pay dirt by acquiring the first 140 acres of what was to become

Picture of original house

the Farm. Twenty or so purchases later (over a number of years), the Farm is roughly 1250 acres and now runs from US 601 on the west to Goodwill Plantation on the east.

That original purchase of 140 acres is where the Farm House is and the first pond, and was acquired for $10 per acre. It runs out to County Road 1285, which is now known as Cate Road. Charlie and Nilla set about constructing a five acre pond and moving a one- room house to the site. The "house" was moved from near where Treye's Pond is today to a site up the creek where the original pond was being constructed. They had a well dug and added electricity and plumbing to what

would become the Farm House. It had a fireplace. The rest of their lives and the lives of their children and grandchildren would revolve around this house and land, which would be continuously expanded and improved as time went by.

Picture of fireplace

In 1950, a living room with another fireplace and a kitchen and dining area were added. The construction was done by a local carpenter named Sam Harris. When Sam was putting the finishing touches on the fireplace, my father asked him "Sam, will that fireplace draw?" Sam replied, "Mr. Charlie, don't let your children anywhere near that fireplace. It will suck them up the chimney!"

Many generations of Cates and their friends have spent untold hours sitting or standing around that fireplace, chatting or enjoying a cocktail or glass of wine. It is an old timey fireplace that is designed to heat more than a room, and it certainly does. Over the years I have heard many comments such as, "Damn Cate, that is the hottest fireplace I have ever seen!"

Phase II picture, circa 1950

In 1953 Charlie and Nilla hired Sam once again to add on again, adding another combination living and sleeping area as well as a second bathroom. A brick patio was also added as well as an outdoor fireplace and barbeque grill.

This part of the house are known as the Brick Rooms. They were also known as the "New Rooms" for the next 40 years. With the enlargement, the family could stay overnight year around, although to begin with, the only heat was from the three fireplaces in the three main rooms. I can assure you that on a cold morning, the children did not get out of bed easily until my father got all three fireplaces going. Eventually,

Phase III picture, circa 1953

some electric heaters were added.

In January, 1962, a fire started in kitchen, caught the curtains on fire and quickly advanced in to the attic of the Farm House. Nilla and my sister Betsy were there and quickly summoned Charlie from outside. Charlie sent Betsy to the store on the highway to call for help. At that time there was no phone in the house, much less a cell phone nearby. While she was gone, Nilla and Charlie set about removing what they could from the house, fully expecting it to quickly burn to the ground. The Eastover Volunteer Fire Department showed up surprisingly fast, as Betsy met them on the road to lead them in. Jimmy Gunter and I were duck hunting in the Duck Pond that afternoon. When I was beginning to realize that I was smelling smoke, I heard the fire truck coming and then hightailed it back upstream to the house. When I arrived, a number of neighbors had followed the fire truck in and were helping to carry things out of the house, as good country neighbors will do.

Miraculously, the house was saved. The fire had been pretty much contained in the attic. The insulation and rafters and the roof had to be replaced, and everything below had to be restored and refinished from the water damage, and within a few months it was as good as new. I believe that those were the last major repairs done to the Farm House until 1988.

Phase IV picture, circa 1988

In 1988, somewhat inspired be the house that Betsy and I had built and moved into the year before, the fourth addition was begun, adding a bedroom and bath to the east end of the house. Also at that time, the kitchen and dining area were moved to the brick rooms, and the old kitchen became a mud room.

Sometime in the early 1950's a small army surplus building was moved from Fort Jackson to just up the hill in the woods behind the main house. It was to be used for children and any friends that might be staying at the Farm. It has forever

Little House now

been called the "Little House" and was a great spot for young boys to hang out. It gave an 8 to 10-year-old boy a great sense of freedom to spend the night up in the Little House. In those days, it was just one frame room with no insulation. It had a light bulb hanging from the ceiling and a spigot outside but no other plumbing. As I said, it quickly became a hangout for the boys. It was almost like being at camp for young boys like Charlie and Billy Cate, Jimmy Gunter, Cantey Haile, George King and many others.

Nilla and Charlie began to spend nearly all their free time at the Farm. All the three children often accompanied them, but since I was the youngest, I was almost always taken along until such time as I could drive. I could usually take a friend along, and my most usual companions were Jimmy Gunter, Donny Wood, Zach McGhee, Billy Bruner or Cal McMeekin. I can tell you it was a wonderful place for a pre-teen boy to discover independence. Endless woods and swamps to explore, always a horse to ride, or countless hours on the pond, whether fishing, swimming, or at night, frog gigging. Nilla did not love cooking frog legs for us for breakfast the next morning, but she would, so long as we cleaned them.

Nilla was a lifelong gardener. Her specialty was native plants and wildflowers. She spent the next 50 years of her life planting and nurturing her plants in the several acres around the house and around the edge of the pond. She was often accompanied on jaunts to the Farm by her dear friends, Anna King, Myrtis Singleton, or Betsy Hane. Her native garden there was the site of many garden club tours and lectures by various "experts".

From the beginning, Charlie wanted the Farm to be sustainable and to pay its own way. With his farming background, that was just the way it was supposed to be. Over the years, just about everything was experimented with. He started with row crops because that is what he knew. Cotton, corn, soybeans and other row crops were all grown at one time or other. A herd of beef cattle was always there for as long as I can remember until about ten years ago. We seasonally had pigs in various numbers. We even had beehives. Charlie was very

Beef cattle

curious about things and always willing to try some new idea. He put in an irrigation system from the pond and created a huge vegetable garden

In the mid 1950s the Soil Bank was created by the United States Department of Agriculture to encourage farmers to take marginal farmland out of row crop production and plant it in either timber or permanent pasture. The farmer entered into a contract with the Soil Conservation Service for ten years and received a cash payment per acre each year for doing so. This popular program accelerated a trend that was already happening across the Southeast. Charlie had already determined that most of our farm was better suited for cattle and timber production than growing commercial crops anyway, so this new program suited his plans perfectly. He started with a purebred Herford herd, but by the early 60s switched to a purebred Angus. The commercial cattle industry began to change in the 1960s and most commercial herds were using crossbred momma cows serviced by a purebred bull. In order to create the most "hybrid vigor", a three-way cross works best. To accomplish this, we would change bull breeds every few years. We used this system for the rest of the time that we were in the cattle business.

Immediately upon acquiring new land Nilla and Charlie would set about to improve what they bought. Much of the existing timber stands had been high graded over the years. This was a practice that was quite common in the old days whereby a stand was logged picking out certain species only and leaving the rest or harvesting the best trees within a species and leaving the inferior ones. Such practices usually leaves a mess that doesn't straighten itself out very well without some type of intervention. In the early days, they relied on Mr. C. W. Hall from the South Carolina Forestry Commission for guidance in renovating the old stands, as well as planting some of the old fields that were being converted from cropland to timberland. Sometime around 1960, consulting forester Bill Milliken got involved, and Buckeye Farms has been a client with Milliken Forestry Company ever since. In 1970, my lifelong friend, Angus Lafaye, was hired as a forester by Milliken, and he then became the Farm's go to guy. More on this relationship later when we get to the chapter on Forestry.

The People Before

Much has been written about the early settlement of central South Carolina as well as the Colonial Period, the Revolutionary Period, the development of the plantation system, slavery, the Civil War and its aftermath. These subjects have been dissected by writers much more talented than I, so I won't try to analyze and dissect further in this book. You will learn far more about these subjects by reading some of reference books that I name in my Introduction. I will use historical references from these periods or events to set up how they shaped the landscape on our Farm and the surrounding neighborhood, as well the people and wildlife who lived there.

By the beginnings of the Colonial period in COWASEE Basin area, the Native Americans that had survived the European diseases for which they had no immunity to had moved further into the backcountry. Many were dead from such diseases such as smallpox or cholera before ever seeing or making contact with a European.

The early development of Lower Richland County was built pretty much around the plantation system which involved large scale agriculture that was very labor intensive with most of the work being done by enslaved Africans. This system set in place the demographics that exist in the rural coastal plain in South Carolina to this day. Let's not kid ourselves. Slavery was a hideous system that ultimately, nobody benefitted from, and in the end, everybody lost. It lasted in South Carolina for 200 years, and once it became entrenched for several generations, there was no good solution to the system that was not going to cause a lot of pain. Obviously, they should have tried a little harder, because the ultimate solution, the American Civil War, was a horrific event, the aftershocks of which can still be felt 150 years later.

I will focus on Goodwill Plantation because it most affected the immediate neighborhood around our Farm. Goodwill was put together by a series of land grants, and by 1785 was owned by Daniel Huger, a wealthy low country planter, who owned several rice plantations on the coast. At one time, Goodwill reached nearly 7500 acres, over twice its size today. The Huger family sold Goodwill to Edward Barnwell Heyward in 1858.

Restored slave cabin at Goodwill

Goodwill operated during ante-bellum times as what was known as a "supply plantation" meaning that in addition to growing cotton, corn, potatoes and other food crops as well as cattle and pigs were produced and sent downstream by boat to provision the owner's single crop rice plantations on the coast. Some rice was produced at Goodwill, especially after it was acquired by the Heywards. Evidence of this is still seen today by the extensive systems of ditches and dikes in the river swamp.

Shortly after the outbreak of the Civil War, Union troops were threatening Heyward's coastal plantations, so he decided to move all his slaves to Goodwill for protection and safekeeping. Prior to the war, there were usually 65 to 70 slaves at Goodwill. By February 1865 there were around 1,000! I find this number to be staggering! Remember that by 1865 there was no money left in South Carolina and very little food or other supplies for anyone. How was it possible to provide for 1000 souls in this environment? I guess the

Mill House at Goodwill by Grover Rye

answer comes from the ingenuity of the slaves themselves. Over the years they had learned to make or grow just about anything, so they relied on their own skills as well as the natural resources of the plantation itself to sustain themselves through the end of the war and its aftermath.

At the end of the war, a union officer came to Goodwill to assemble the slaves and tell them they were free. The scene is described in *Seed from Madagascar* on page 138 and I quote:

About the middle of 1865 my father drove from his Goodwill plantation to Columbia and returned with a Federal officer with him in his buggy. The Negroes were all called together, and the officer, standing in the buggy in their midst, made them a speech. During the speech he told them they were free and could come and go as they pleased.

Okay, what now? The scene is further described below:

I have often wondered how the Negroes received this announcement. I have asked Mr. Jones[1] particularly what happened, and also a brother of mine that was old enough to remember. Both told me the Negroes did nothing. There was no demonstration on their part, according to these two eyewitnesses. All they remembered was that the Negroes loafed the rest of the day, talking among themselves and probably speculating as to when they would return to the Combahee[2]. The next day, Mr. Jones persuaded them to return to work, on the promise of my father and grandfather that the matter of remuneration would be arranged. The crop had been planted, and it was to the interest of all that it should be cultivated and harvested. In fact, it was all that stood between both whites and blacks, and starvation.

Remember, South Carolina had trapped itself in this system for 200 years, many, many generations. In 1865 many of the white Carolinians were illiterate, and nearly all the black population was. So, in the rural countryside, they did what they knew how to do. They continued to farm and practiced the skills that they had acquired. This really brings us to the main theme of my story, which covers from the end of the Civil War and the changes that occur from the onset of Reconstruction to the present time (roughly 150 years). The collapse in the plantation system created a watershed transformation on farms throughout South Carolina and across the Southeast and had a huge impact on the people and wildlife that lived on those farms.

When the war ended and the Reconstruction period began, the plantation system which was dependent on slavery had to be completely replaced. What followed was a combination of tenant farming and sharecropping to get the land worked. Sharecroppers typically lived on and worked what I have always called a "one horse farm", representing what one man and a mule (or horse) can work in one years' time, generally thought of in terms of about 40 acres.

After the 1865 crops were harvested at Goodwill, most of the former slaves from the Combahee plantations returned there, where they would fashion a similar lifestyle to those that remained at Goodwill and the surrounding countryside. The landscape became a patchwork of these little one-horse farms. In some cases, former slaves were granted title to their land by their former owners, or they simply rented (tenant farmers) from the owners, or they farmed for the owner on shares (sharecropper). Our farm was no exception, and it too became a patchwork of these small farms. On our roughly 1250 acres, I could take you to probably 15 different homesites, long since abandoned.

These subsistence farmers had a very hard life. They pretty much survived on what they produced or made. The only real cash crop was cotton, and assuming that they made a crop, might provide a few hundred dollars to carry them to the next year. They had a mule or horse, a milk cow, a few chickens, and a garden. The typical house was a one or two room house with no plumbing. Electricity did not reach many of them until after World War II. Seventy years ago, when my father was putting our farm together, most of the tracts had an old house on them, usually abandoned. Today, one of those old houses would be considered a treasure. But in those days, they were considered junk and promptly torn down, and the lumber used for something else. Many of these old houses had some very fine heart pine wood in them.

Most of these houses did not have wells, but instead got their water from springs that often served several families. I mentioned 15 or so homesites on our Farm, and I know of only two old wells. The rest used the half dozen springs, some of which continued to be used into the 1950s. I remember distinctly as a boy in the mid-fifties, watching a mule-drawn wagon come to our spring where our old horse barn is, filling two 55-gallon drums with water and returning back up the road with their weeks supply of water. There is a spring on the east side of our place known as the Edmunds Spring that at one time serviced as many as six families.

These springs were made serviceable to provide drinking water by digging them out to a depth of about two feet in a

Sharecropper House by David Hartfield

square hole about two feet by two feet, and then lining the walls of the square with a wooden box. Once it settled, it provided a reliable source of clear, cool drinking water. The Edmunds Spring had long been abandoned by the time I knew it, but it was still functional, and I remember well as a boy, that while bird hunting , always stopping for a drink when we got to the spring. That is of course, if one of the bird dogs wasn't cooling off in it when we got there!

A partially restored box spring

1. Mr. Jones was the foreman at Goodwill for the Heywards.

2. Most of the slaves at Goodwill at the end of the war had come from the Combahee River Plantations.

The Land Before

Most of us are unaware how much the South Carolina landscape has changed since the first Europeans arrived more than 450 years ago. When Hernando Desoto, the Spanish explorer came through what is now South Carolina in 1540 he found a landscape that was almost entirely wooded except for small patches the Native Americans scratched out for corn and other crops. Of course, wildfires burned large swaths at a time. The Indians intentionally set many fires both as a hunting technique and to help clear areas for crops or camps. Lightening also caused many fires, and these fires burned until the next rain or until it hit a river or a stream that it couldn't cross. Because of the long growing season and the plentiful rainfall, the forests quickly restored themselves, often in an improved condition.

Historically, the South Carolina woodlands have remained roughly evenly divided between hardwood and pine, with the individual species varying, depending on location. When our Farm and the surrounding neighborhoods were first being settled, all land was wooded and had to be cleared by manpower and horsepower before any agriculture could take place or structures built. This had to have been truly brutal work. At the time this was happening, the dominant pine species was longleaf which produced a very high-quality lumber that most of the early buildings were made from. Over the next 200 plus years and by the early 1900s the landscape that was not in a floodplain had become mostly cleared for agriculture.

Also, by 1900, the logging and lumber business had become very active across the Southeast, and those forests that had not been cleared to make way for farms were being targeted for the saw. The biggest problem at this time though was that the logging industry was not yet supported by any scientific forestry. Many of the operators moved through the countryside with small, mobile sawmills, cut out an area and moved to the next site. All reforestation efforts were simply left to Mother Nature. These fairly primitive operations also tended to practice "high grading", which meant that they were targeting certain species within a forest, or targeting the best trees within a species, and then leaving the rest. This high grading practice tended to leave a mess that took a long time to straighten itself out, if ever. The most valuable wood was sought out first. In our neighborhood the longleaf pines were the first to go in the upland areas, and in the river swamp it was the bald cypress being targeted first. By the late 1920s, there were very few woodlands or swamps that had not been cut.

After the Civil War, the farmers, white and black, continued doing the only thing they knew to do - FARM. Of course they farmed what they knew to farm - COTTON. As stated, by the beginning of the Twentieth Century, much of the upland forest had been cleared for agriculture. By the second decade, when the price of cotton began to drop, they simply cleared more land and planted more cotton. I find it amazing that in 1900 the largest cotton producing county in South Carolina was Fairfield, followed by Chester. It is said that you could look from horizon to horizon and see nothing but cotton! This is especially amazing when you think that today there is probably not a single field in either of those counties that contains more than 100 acres. When wandering those counties today, you don't have to look hard to find the devastation to the environment caused by these primitive, unscientific agricultural practices. The steep slopes eroded quickly, causing gulley's (now called ravines) that you could hide a house in, much less a car. Our Farm in Richland County was no exception. The same practices were taking place, and although the slopes weren't as steep, the same mistakes were being made, and the lack of good agricultural practices was taking its toll. It is not hard to find the evidence of these failing farms across the landscape throughout South Carolina, including our Farm.

The subsistence farming system that evolved after the Civil War remained pretty much as is for the next 50 years and then slowly began to change. Up until then, these struggling farmers stayed where they were simply because there were no other options available. The textile industry in South Carolina was growing rapidly by then and was offering some alternatives to at least the poor white farmers. However, it was not much of an alternative, as these early manufacturing jobs provided long hours in poor working conditions for low wages. Industrial jobs in the north slowly began to attract southern farmers especially among African-Americans. What began as a trickle, became a migration by the 1920s and 30s as the agricultural economy in the south collapsed. Abandoned farms began to appear as this trend continued, and land prices plummeted. Fallow fields gradually reverted back to woodlands.

By the 1930s, savvy investors began to sense some long-term opportunity in the very depressed land values in South Carolina and began to piece together large land holdings, many times at only a few dollars per acre. The paper-making industry began manufacturing paper in the South, and by the end of the 1930s had built several large paper mills in South Carolina and began to acquire huge blocks of land on which to grow timber to supply the mills. They found many eager sellers at very depressed prices. Much of the land around our Farm became part of this process. The old farms began to be converted from fallow fields and severely cutover forest into what was to become known as industrial forest land that was at least supported by intensive scientific forestry. So, over the course of less than 100 years, the land around our Farm, and including our Farm, had been almost completely cleared for agriculture or lumber, and now was converting back into mostly woodlands. Many times, a terraced hillside, which is quite common, is the only thing to tell the average observer that the mature forest they are standing in was once something else. And really not very long ago in the overall scheme of things.

The People Now

Most things are still the same in our part of Richland County. It is mostly the same as I remember as a little boy, and you can go eight or ten miles in any direction and find it to still be pretty much the case. That is actually true of all of the COWASEE Basin, which I will get into more in the chapter that covers that very important conservation initiative.

Not only does it look and feel the same, but it is inhabited by mostly the same families that have been there for many generations. Of course, some have left the area, and some have moved into it. If you were to look at a census for the neighborhood around our Farm in 1900, many of the family names would be the same as today. Harris, Wider, Higgins, Fleming, Flemming, Simons, Patterson, Murray, Edmonds, Campbell, Scott, Clarkson, Rye, McLemore, Pressley, and many others that I would call old Eastover names, but I am trying to give examples of close by neighbors whose ancestors were here in 1900. Many of these family names represent black families, some white, and some both. Of course some families

Eight of the 13 Harris children circa 1952

have simply left the scene. I would imagine that if you travelled through most of South Carolina's rural coastal plain, that you see much the same pattern and demographics.

The biggest difference between now and 1900 is that back then the ancestors of the families mentioned above were scattered all over the countryside trying to make a living farming. By mid-century, very few were actually farming, and many had moved away, and those that remained tended to settle in small neighborhoods (often family neighborhoods), and developed trades and other forms of employment.

Sandhill Mercantile circa 1990 by Jack Pringle

Another difference is that there used to be a country store every several miles along the roads, harking back to the day that people had to ride a horse or wagon to get there. Or walk. Today, there are almost no stores that last long between Columbia and Sumter, or even less between St. Matthews and

Camden, both a distance of around 40 miles. In fact, there is only one place between St. Matthews and I-20 south of Camden on US 601 that you could buy a gallon of gas or a soft drink. I find it amazing that there are no open stores but one for 40 miles on a US highway when almost the whole route is within 25 miles of Columbia. A couple of notable exceptions to this trend are Mr. Bunky's and Horse and Garden. Mr. Bunky's is truly a classic country store that features almost everything from a popular restaurant, to a hardware store, to a meat market (with deer processing as a side), a grocery store, and a flea market upstairs where you can find anything from a toilet seat to a wagon harness. Bunky's restaurant is always busy at breakfast and lunch with a pleasant mix of locals, hunters and fishermen, and military, since it is next door to the thriving McEntire National Guard Base.

Mr. Bunky's Store

If you go back toward Columbia a few miles to Horrell Hill, you will find Horse and Garden Ace Hardware, which is a particularly clean, well-stocked hardware and feed store with good service and reasonable prices.

Horse and Garden

Margaret's

Another popular eatery is Margaret's, which serves breakfast and lunch every day but Monday, and provides a folksy, friendly atmosphere again made up of locals, hunters and fishermen, and military, particularly on drill weekends.

Good Hope Baptist Church

Why are there so few business's that are successful along these long and busy stretches of highway? Well my own theory is that almost everyone on those highways is going somewhere, and in a hurry to get there, and their schedule doesn't include a stop on the way. The establishments just mentioned have a reputation for good food or being well stocked and likely to attract someone from the road to stop and pick up supplies or a quick bite on the way to the Wateree River, Santee Lakes, or going to the beach. Of course, there is the obvious appeal to the locals, and for me, it is hard to make it through a day, much less a weekend without hitting one or more of the establishments.

Over the last 50 or 60 years or so, country churches have suffered much the same fate as country stores and for many of the same reasons. Once the membership drops below a certain level, it is hard to keep the doors open.

Despite some these physical changes, the general flavor remains the same. The same families have been our neighbors for as long as I can remember. It looks the same and it feels the same. That is, if you stay off the highway. That is clearly different. There is a whole lot more traffic, way more than just 10 or 15 years ago!

The Land Now

As previously stated, all but about 100 acres of our roughly 1250 acres is in forest under varying degrees of management. Remember that 100 years ago that the vast majority of this land was cleared and in agriculture, with the primary crop being cotton, plus some corn, potatoes and other food crops for consumption. Also remember, that 100 years prior to that, this same 1250 acres was all woodlands. Amazing, when you think about it.

As stated earlier, it was always Charlie's intention to have the Farm completely support itself. After trying just about every crop that will grow in our part of the world in order to make the farm operation productive, he concluded by the late 1950s that forestry would produce the most amount of income with the least investment over the long haul. From that point forward, very few crops were grown commercially, and the few crops that were grown, were grown for wildlife or to support the beef cattle herd that was maintained until just a few years ago. Also remember that Charlie generally raised varying numbers of pigs as well, so some corn was grown to support them as well as the dove hunting hobby. Curiously, in those days, deer, which were becoming much more plentiful by then, did not seem to care about the corn.

Charlie and Nilla both liked to wing shoot (as did their children), so Charlie always planted a dove field in those days with sporadic success, and bobwhite quail (birds) were still fairly plentiful, so he focused his wildlife efforts in that direction. Around 1960 Charlie got the idea to ditch and dike one of the row crop fields and create a duck pond of about five acres that could be flooded to a shallow depth from a pond that was constructed up stream known as "The Pond in the Woods". At the time of its construction, our duckpond was one of the first man-made flooded waterfowl impoundments along the Wateree. Today, there may be as many as 75. Over the years our family and friends have certainly had a good time with the duck pond. Like most duck ponds, it has provided mixed results, but several generations of Cates or cousins, or friends, have killed their first duck there.

Duck Pond

Getting back to forestry, it was always Charlie's goal to make our forest totally sustainable, meaning that he could harvest a part of a certain percentage of the Farm each year, and by the time he had worked all the way through it, it would be time to start the process over without the Farm ever looking "cut over". Although Charlie did not live long enough to see the Farm totally sustainable, and probably never heard the buzzword "sustainable forestry", but that is exactly what he was trying to accomplish. Today, because of his and Nilla's foresight, that is indeed the way that the present generation is able to manage the forest today.

As previously stated, they already had a relationship with Bill Milliken at Milliken Forestry Company, and by the time I got actively involved in the process, my lifelong friend, Angus Lafaye was working at Milliken and had taken us on as a client. I believe that the foresters at Milliken, as well as the professionals at the various agricultural and forestry agencies truly enjoyed working at our farm. Charlie and Nilla listened to their advice and worked diligently to implement their recommended practices. Always willing to try something different, Charlie was a sponge for new information to help improve his ever-expanding forest. Recognizing them for their efforts and innovations, Charlie and Nilla were recognized in 1979 by the Tree Farm Committee and the South Carolina Forestry Association as South Carolina's "Tree Farmer of the Year"!

Nilla and Charlie with Tree Farm Award 1979

Any time that I am advising a landowner, or a prospective landowner, about land management, I always stress the importance of deciding exactly what it is that you want to accomplish with your land. Is it income or recreation? Hunting and fishing? Investment quality? Beauty? Peace and quiet? You can make it any of those things, or you can make it all of them. You can certainly have multiple objectives, and should have, but they need to be prioritized in order to keep your eyes on the main target. I like to use our own place as an example. We operate our farm with three main priorities in the following order: 1) Timber production, 2) Wildlife management, and 3) aesthetics. Since we are trying to pay all of our bills at the Farm with forest products proceeds, we need to intensively manage our forest to maximize income. That said, we never make a management decision without considering all three priorities. We might not do a forestry project that makes perfectly good forestry sense simply because we don't think it will look good. Another landowner may have a completely different set of priorities. The income part of it might not be important, and it all might be about looking good or maximizing hunting and fishing opportunities. The important thing as a landowner is to recognize what it is that you are trying to accomplish. I never cease to be amazed by second and third generation landowners that have no plan for their land whatsoever, even though that land may be their family's most valuable asset!

Planting duck pond 2018

Clearly, there are some parts of the property that our priorities might apply more than others. And there are a few areas that we simply don't include in our management plan at all, and we leave those areas simply to Mother Nature because of their beauty. A casual ride-through could be made, and one might not notice how intensively we manage certain parts of the Farm. And we do indeed manage aggressively in certain areas. We have to if we intend to let the wood products proceeds carry the load of our expenses.

We don't hesitate to use a "clear cut" if that is the prescription that maximizes production. That said, we think carefully about the location of a clear cut and prefer that the size be in the 30 to 40 acre range and not exceed 50 acres. The ideal location for a clear cut is in a part of the Farm that most family members or guests would never even see in their regular comings and goings. The great thing about growing trees in this part of the world is that they grow really fast with plenty of rainfall and long growing seasons. If a site is properly prepared and followed by planting high quality improved loblolly seedlings it is amazing how fast one forgets that it even was a clear-cut in the first place. On a good site, one should expect to get a first commercial thinning in 12 to 15 years, and then

Charlie Pringle in five-year-old loblolly stand following clearcut

a second one five to seven years after that. What you do after that goes back to what your individual management objectives for your property happen to be. In our case, we may get a third or fourth thinning before doing a final harvest and starting the process over.

These small clear-cuts (under 50 acres) also offer a boon to wildlife of all stripes for the first five or six years, creating a great edge effect and starting the plant secession growth all over again when the sunlight hits the freshly disturbed soil. This creates the development of lush and succulent weed growth of many different legumes and browse that provide nutritious food and good cover for the various edge animals such as deer, turkey, quail, rabbits and many others. The sudden openings provide a great attractant for numerous species of songbirds as well.

In the mid 1980s Milliken Forestry hired Gordon Baker as a young forester, and he was soon assigned to work with Angus Lafaye to help him manage the various properties under his management. Our farm soon became one of his responsibilities. We quickly became friends and have always worked well together, primarily I think because we pretty much view the forest through the same lens. He and Angus have always understood what our objectives were, so there have been almost no misunderstandings when we undertook a particular forestry project. We have tried a lot of experiments over the years, and we've discovered many that work, and more importantly, those that don't work. We have been through Hurricane Hugo together in 1989, and the great flood of 2015. Both of those catastrophic events completely knocked us out of our long-term management plan, and required a short term change of priorities. The impact of both of these storms was felt on the Farm for many years.

Let me say this right now. If you are a timberland owner of more than just a few acres, your most important and trusted advisor when it comes to your land should be your forester. It's not your lawyer. It's not your accountant. It's not your financial advisor. It is your forester! I know this to be a fact. I will say further, that if you don't have that kind of personal relationship with your forester, then you have the wrong forester!

Within the last 30 to 40 years, there has been a vigorously renewed interest in reestablishing longleaf pines to its original range which at one time was primarily the coastal plain across the Southeast from southeastern Virginia to east Texas. This renewed interest is across a broad front and includes conservationists, foresters, landowners, and various agencies within the federal and state governments. When the Europeans first began exploring the Southeast in the early 1500s, longleaf was the dominant tree species on approximately 90 million acres in the range described above. By the mid-twentieth century the longleaf range had been depleted by more than 97 percent. Obviously, it was going to take a coordinated effort to stop this decline and keep longleaf from just completely disappearing. Only in the last few years has the loss of acreage ended and actually has begun to increase.

Why was the longleaf range so depleted in the first place? Well, for starters, longleaf was the superior pine species in the range. Its wood is very dense and heavy with sap called rosin and produced a very high-quality lumber that would last unpainted almost indefinitely. Also, the rosin could be withdrawn from the trees and used as a byproduct to produce many useful products such as turpentine, tar and pitch used in the caulking of wooden ship hulls as well as waterproofing the many ropes used on those ships. As the longleaf stands were removed from land like ours, those acres not cleared for agriculture seeded in for the most part with loblolly, a pine species that reproduces itself much more aggressively than longleaf, and loblolly soon became the dominant pine species in the second generation forest of the former longleaf range.

Our Farm retained a few residual stands of longleaf, and about 30 years or so ago we started to pay attention to the longleaf "story" and to its dramatic decline and we decided to do what we could to reverse the decline at least on our land. In the longleaf stands that still existed, although mixed with loblolly in an area of maybe 200 acres, Gordon and I determined that going forward that we would manage that area with an uneven age management strategy and continuously favoring the longleaf in the process. This meant that we would never have a final harvest in that area, and that when we thinned, we would favor the longleaf, and remove the loblolly as it made sense to do so. This strategy doesn't mean that we won't ever cut a longleaf. Quite the opposite. We are still in this for the money, so when thinning we will remove certain trees to make way for a young sapling trying to break into the overstory. We would complement that with an aggressive prescribed fire program to eliminate the loblolly seedlings that volunteered as well as other hardwood competition. Fire will kill a loblolly seedling if under about three feet tall, whereas longleaf is a fire dependent species, which means fire is very important to its life cycle.

Prescribed fire in progress

We have used prescribed fire in certain parts of our woodlands for nearly 50 years. When we first started using fire, we were more concerned with controlling the fire, and did not worry much about the smoke. Many times, we would often follow a blustery February day with an all-night burn, as the fire is much easier to handle at night. We would not even consider using that strategy today and would run the risk of getting in trouble if we did. That is because of the smoke. At night an inversion usually occurs and causes the smoke to settle and can create quite a hazard out on the highways, especially if a little fog mixes with it. There is so much more traffic on the roads today that everyone is much more concerned about where their smoke is going to go. As we gained experience with our burning program, we learned a lot about predicting fire behavior. One should plan their burn based on a combination of three factors: temperature, wind, and humidity. Also, conditions can really change over the course of a burn day. As the temperature rises, and the humidity drops, it can go from being too wet to too dry in a hurry. The fire does need to be hot enough to accomplish the mission, however.

We have also converted several loblolly stands to longleaf following a clear-cut of the loblolly. That is not nearly as easy as it sounds however, as the loblolly seeds remain persistent on the ground as well as constant seeding in from around the edges. To be successful requires a strong herbicide treatment to start with on the site, and maybe a release treatment when the seedlings begin to grow. A prescribed fire regimen every two to three years should keep most of the loblolly out.

Okay, I love the longleaf pine! It is my favorite native conifer! It is truly a majestic tree that has many wonderful qualities. It produces a very high-quality lumber. It is fire resistant, ice storm resistant (once it reaches a certain size), fairs better in

Uneven age longleaf forest

high winds, drought resistant, and it is bug resistant. All this, and its beautiful to look at, and it makes wonderful music when the wind rustles through its needles. All this said, what's not to like? Well, it grows really slowly and it is hard to establish. It does live a very long time, 300 or more years, while a loblolly rarely sees 100 years. We have concluded that it does not make good economic sense, given our objectives, to devote any more of our acreage than we do to longleaf production. I just don't believe that we can meet our sustainability goals with longleaf. Everything simply takes too long. In the meantime, we will continue to try to improve the quality of the longleaf stands that we have. This view could change if at some point genetic improvements are made to the longleaf species that allow it to compete economically with the loblolly.

Our family is very proud of the beauty of our woodlands. It represents several generations of diligent management and has proven to be a reliable source of income for many years. The Farm has been publicly recognized over the years for its management practices. In 2015, it was selected as South Carolina's Tree Farm of the Year by the SC Tree Farm Committee and the Forestry Association of South Carolina!

It is the second time that our farm has won this same award as Nilla and Charlie were the award winner back in 1979. To my knowledge, it is the only time that a farm in South Carolina has won this same award twice. I think that is really cool. I think that my parents would also think its pretty cool.

Tree Farm Award

The Family

You have already met Nilla and Charlie (my parents) and you will continue to hear from them throughout this story, but this chapter is going to be devoted primarily to the rest of us. Since I am the one writing this book, I will start with my family.

What I describe as an extraordinarily happy marriage of 53 years began with a very fun and romantic summer job in Vermont when Betsy and I were in college. We were both working at a resort called the Tyler Place on Lake Champlain in northern Vermont. We actually knew each other before going to Vermont, as we both had gone to Dreher High School in Columbia but were in different classes. We weren't really friends but shared some peripheral friends. We had not seen each other since Betsy had graduated from High School three years earlier and gone off to college at Mary Baldwin College in Staunton, Virginia. I graduated a year later and headed off to college at Clemson University. There was a common denominator as to why we both ended up in the same place that summer. We had a mutual friend, Karen Espendahl, that had worked at the Tyler Place the previous summer. She loved it and applied for and was given the horseback and riding management position for the next year. Karen's bigger-than-life personality had gotten her the job, and pretty quickly she realized that she was going to need some help managing the horses. She quickly contacted everyone that she knew that knew anything about horses. She contacted Betsy Walker, JoeMac Bates (who was my life-long friend) and subsequently myself, and urged us all to apply for riding instructor jobs at the Tyler Place.

Betsy and JoeMac got the jobs as Karen's assistants, but I was hired for an unknown position on the staff. I assumed that I would be a waiter in the dining room or maybe a position at the waterfront. At any rate, I was happy to have been offered a job and was looking forward to a great adventure. The Tyler Place has been in business and owned by the same family since 1933. In the 50's, 60's, and 70's they hired about 75 or so college students to staff the resort each summer. At that time, most of the clientele was from the Northeast, so the Tyler's tried to bring in as many southern boys and girls as possible because the New Englanders loved the southern manners. Today, they look for the same age class, but with more of an international flavor. The world is a lot smaller than it was in 1964, and the guests are likely to be from almost anywhere in America.

JoeMac and I drove up in early June, 1964. Our longtime friends, Margaret Bell and Susan Rigby accompanied us on the journey, as Karen had also helped them get jobs at the Tyler Place. Like me, they did not know what their jobs would be. The trip up was quite an adventure itself, especially for a carload of naïve southern girls and boys. We stopped in Washington for several days and then spent several more days in New York, before heading up the west bank of the Hudson River into northern New York before crossing back across the Hudson into southern Vermont. It was a wonderful time. When we arrived at the Tyler Place I was immediately assigned to the waterfront to assemble the boat docks and rafts that have to be taken up each fall because of the ice that encloses all of Lake Champlain. It was about 60 degrees all day, and the water temperature was mid 50s I would guess, and we spent the next three day's in the water assembling the docks and rafts. I can tell you, working in the dining room as a waiter was beginning to look pretty good to this southern boy!

I actually trained for half a day as a waiter before being assigned to be co-director for the Sub Teens (10-12 year old's). My Partner was a girl from New York named Clare Tweedy, who was actually Mrs. Tyler's niece. We hit it right off, and have remained friends since. She and her husband still live in New York, and we often see them when we visit the Tyler Place.

What does any of this side track about the Tyler Place have to do with the Farm? Well, I'm getting ready to tell you. About Easter in the spring of 1964, my parents got my mid-term grades from Clemson, and I was flunking calculus for the second time. My father announced to me while I was home on break that if I flunked calculus, I would not be going to Vermont, but would be going to summer school instead. I am not sure whether anything could have motivated me to do better in calculus, but I sure

Betsy with General Lee at the Tyler Place 1964

spent a lot of time worrying about it over the next few weeks. My grades came in three days before time to leave. D minus!!! We are off!! As the next several paragraphs will tell you, I have spent the rest of my life thinking that the D- in calculus was the best and most important grade that I made in college! I cannot begin to imagine how different my life might have turned out if I had flunked calculus and had to go to summer school and not gone to the Tyler Place! It was truly one of those forks in the road of life. If I had taken the other one, who knows?

The first night at the Tyler Place I saw Betsy Walker. We spent some time visiting and talking about friends we knew from high school. Over the next week or so, we found ourselves in the same group when we went out after work. Sometimes we would go to Phillipsburg, a village across the border in Quebec,

Bandstand Island at the Tyler Place 2019

hanging out as a group and drinking some Canadian beer. Molson was the beer of choice that summer. Every ten days to two weeks or so a group would pile into several cars and go to Montreal (about 50 miles away) after work, not leaving until after 10 PM. These excursions were all night affairs, hitting as many bars as possible and then going somewhere for a plate of Chinese food or a big breakfast to help with the drive back to the Tyler Place in order to get there in time for work that day.

By this time, although we were mostly doing social activities in groups, Betsy and I were usually paired together, and I started to get the feeling that she might be getting interested in me. I know that I was getting interested in her! I remember exactly where we were and what we were doing when we shared our first real kiss. I remember the thought going through my mind: "Don't mess this up, Cate!" For the rest of that magical summer, when we were not working, we were virtually always together.

1964 was the height of the "Animal House" years across college campuses, and the setting at the Tyler Place afforded a very diverse group of college kids a chance to showcase some of their skills. I would not begin to tell readers everything that happened that summer, but I will share one episode that particularly stands out. Pixley Tyler, Ed and Judy Tyler's daughter was traveling in Europe that summer, so they hired a manager to run the staff in her place. The "manager" was really just a few years older than we were and was more than a little enamored with the power of his new position. He insisted that the staff call him Mr. Ballou instead of Bill. The Tyler's had given him the use of Pixley's car for the summer, a classic red Triumph TR4 sports car. This went to his head also, and that plus the fact that he didn't mind hitting on the girls on staff further alienated him from the staff, especially the guys. There weren't any serious issues. Just enough to give the staff something to grumble about, or make jokes about. The staff ate its meals in a separate dining room from the guests in the Inn. The food was good, and a bunch of 20 year old's could eat a lot of it. We also could drink a lot of milk. At some point the kitchen staff complained to "Mr." Ballou that the staff was drinking too much of overall milk supply. So what did Ballou do? He cut off all milk to the staff! This really got the staff riled! I mean, here we are in the heart of dairy country, and he cuts off our milk ration. In truth, we weren't worried about milk. We were worried about beer! That said, it gave us a "cause" to rally around, and by mid-morning, we had decided that we were going to fix that SOB! That afternoon a plan was developed, and about three in the morning the next day a group of about 15 of us met in the road by the Tyler Cottage where Ballou had an apartment. We took the TR-4 out of gear and rolled it 1/2 mile up the road to where the 150 year old inn stood. When we got to the front steps, we surrounded the car, lifted it up and then carried it up the steps, rolled it through the front door and down the hall to the formal dining room. We were very proud! We had pulled off the perfect covert operation.

We took a few pictures for posterity, complete with protest signs, and left. Two things were noticeable the next morning when I showed up for work. First, the milk machine in the staff dining room was flowing full tilt, and second, the car was gone

Triumph in Tyler Place dining room during milk protest

from the dining room. I guess the kitchen staff removed it when they came in a couple of hours before the rest of us. At any rate, nobody in management ever mentioned the incident to the staff, and to my knowledge, it was never figured out just who had pulled off the prank, and nobody was even questioned about it to my knowledge. I know that I was not. The event remains legendary at the Tyler Place to this day!

As this magical summer was coming to an end, we couldn't help but wonder how things would work out when we left the Tyler Place. Betsy would be headed back to school in

Virginia, and I would be headed back to Clemson. At least we were from the same town, so we at least would be in the same place for holidays. Everybody else that had paired up for the summer were headed back to Anywhere, USA, and most would never see each other again. One thing that did happen when we got home from the Tyler Place before we both headed back to school was that Betsy was introduced to the Farm for the first time. She had heard me bragging about it all summer. She was also introduced to my parents, Nilla and Charlie, and met the new horse that Charlie had purchased that summer. He was a paint gelding named Patches. Nilla and Charlie were thrilled that Betsy was a skilled rider and interested in the Farm. Nilla and Charlie both enjoyed riding and still rode some, so Betsy's strong interest and my renewed interest inspired them to purchase three more horses over the next year's time. The first

Billy and Buck spring 1965

Betsy at Cooks Mountain with me on picnic trail ride circa 1965.

Penny and Buck late summer 1965

one was Penny, an appaloosa mare that was bred when we got her. She had her foal early in the winter of 1964, a colt that we named Buck.

The next two were Rocky, a bred quarter horse mare and an older quarter horse mare named Lady. Betsy's and my parents already knew each other and both seemed very pleased with the choices we had made in Vermont.

Obviously, the long-distance relationship did work out in our case. I made several trips to Mary Baldwin that year, and Betsy made several to Clemson. Betsy graduated the next spring and took a job teaching school in Atlanta while I was finishing my degree at Clemson. That was a lot closer than Mary Baldwin, so it was easier to see each other during the school year. We became engaged over Christmas break in 1965 with plans to be married in late summer 1966. I graduated in May of 1966, and in early June reported to Fort Bragg, North Carolina, where I spent most of the rest of the summer. I came home August 1st as a new second lieutenant in the Air Defense Artillery Branch in the United States Army. It was a whirlwind next few days before Betsy and I were married on August 6, 1966. We honeymooned at my sister Betsy's new house at Lake Toxaway, North Carolina.

Billy and Betsy August 6, 1966 at Trinity Church in Columbia

We had about a month to kill before reporting to my next duty station, Fort Bliss in El Paso, Texas. Fort Bliss is where the Air Defense Artillery School was located, and where I was to receive the Officer Basic Course and my MOS (Military Occupational Specialty) training. While we were waiting to report, Nilla and Charlie gave us permission to live in the Farm House. This was an especially fun time for us, hanging out, learning to keep house, working in a little fishing, a little deer hunting, and riding horses. This is probably about when we first began to seriously discuss living at the Farm when we returned from the military.

Billy as an army officer circa 1968

The next two years passed surprisingly fast. We loved our time at Fort Bliss. El Paso is in the high desert in far west Texas with an altitude of about 4000 feet. The climate is sunny, dry, and for the most part pleasant. We both felt that it was a great experience for a young couple to be completely on our own and forced to just figure out how to make things work without running home to ask one of our parents. Remember, in those days a long-distance phone call was a big deal. Almost all communication was done by mail. We had two dogs that we dearly loved (Amos, a Labrador, and Rebel, a beagle), and we doted on them constantly. Not much has changed there, I guess. More on that later. At any rate, we made some great friends with other young couples in similar circumstances, acquired a taste for Mexican food and cheap Mexican whiskey, and generally made the most of our time in the Army.

Before our separation from the service in September 1968, two significant events occurred. First, Betsy became pregnant with our first born, Walker. Secondly, we purchased a house, sight unseen, back in Columbia. A friend let Betsy know about the fact that it was going to be available, and it was a house that I was vaguely familiar with as a friend of mine had grown up there. We told our mothers about it, and they went by, took many pictures, and they agreed that it was a nice starter home. So, we made the deal through letters and a couple of phone calls without ever setting foot in it. My, how times have changed.

We left El Paso with mixed emotions, knowing that we had shared a wonderful experience together, and had gained a lot of life lessons being completely on our own. The army had really been good for me I know. At the same time, we had missed our family and friends in South Carolina, and we were anxious to get on with our lives. We were especially looking forward to getting to the Farm, which was probably the one thing that we missed most about being gone for two years. Up until the time that we had bought the house on Belmont, we had continued to talk about moving to the Farm as soon it was practical to do so.

The army was to remove our furniture and household goods and ship it to us in about six weeks after we left Fort Bliss. So, we loaded what we thought we might need for the next month or so into our 1965 Plymouth Valiant, along with our two dogs, Amos and Rebel, and our cat, Bliss who had never been in a car before, and headed east for the 2,000 mile trip home. Needless to say, it was an interesting three days. Remember that Betsy was four months pregnant! The most memorable part was the cat, Bliss, who had disappeared for three days when the movers showed up and we were staying with friends. We kept going by the house looking for Bliss to no avail and were concluding that we were going to have to leave her. She showed up just before we left and we put her in a crate, which she also had never been in, said our goodbyes, picked up I-10 and headed home. Well, Bliss did not think much of being in the car, much less the crate and began to squall. I took it for about an hour, and then said, "Open that damn crate." That didn't work so hot either, as Bliss took off running around the inside of the car, banking off all the windows as she went. So, back into the crate she went, and immediately back to squalling. After another hour, we let her out again only to have her take off banking off all the windows including the windshield. It was all I could do not to open my window when she came by the driver's side, sending her into the desert in west Texas.

She eventually settled down, and three days later we arrived back in Columbia, spending a few days visiting our parents before moving into our new home. We would live in three different houses over the next 20 years before realizing our dream to build our own house at the Farm. More on this later.

House on Belmont

John Walker Cate was born March 3, 1969, and life quickly became very busy! I was immersed in trying to establish my career at our family business, Cate-McLaurin Company, and Betsy was busy taking care of a baby and learning to run a household.

Even though we established routines, life was still busy, and as we would learn, became more so, as our second child, Nilla Perry Cate was born on November 6, 1972. We moved into a larger house the next year, and from a practical standpoint, ideas of moving to the Farm had moved to the back burner.

Elizabeth Finley Cate was born October 3, 1976, and all who know Elizabeth, know that life got really busy. As busy as things became, the Farm remained the center point in my life. I was kind of commuting in reverse as most all of my free time was spent at the Farm.

The family spent a lot of time there also as we frequently spent vacations or long weekends there with friends. My parents were still in good health and were usually there several days a week. My mother, Nilla, always prepared Sunday lunch, and all Cates had a standing invitation. Our crowd of five were nearly always there. Many Sundays my brother Charlie's family would be there, and several times a year my sister Betsy's would be, so often there were lots of cousins to play with. It was a wonderful family tradition.

Famiy adults eating Sunday lunch circa early 1980s
Left to right Betsy Cate Pringle, Billy, Charlie, Charlie, Betsy,
Johnny Pringle, Audrey, Nilla

Life remained busy. In addition to the stresses of trying to run a business, I continued my deep involvement in the

Farm, and took over more and more of the management duties as my parents, Nilla and Charlie, began to age. I was the one of the three siblings that really took to it, and that had been the case since childhood. Walker took to it also, and usually accompanied me, just as I had with my parents as a very young child. He started hunting and fishing at a very young age, and frequently went with me or his grandfather. By the time he was nine he was fishing on his own regularly, and had killed his first deer.

My parents had started a unique tradition in the swimming hole in the pond with my siblings. First they taught us to swim. When you could jump off the end of the dock and swim to the bank, you were awarded your first fishing rod. After that, when you could jump off the dock, and swim to the swimming raft, perhaps 100 feet away, you were awarded a tackle box. And then, when you could jump off the dock and swim to the other side of the pond, you were awarded the privilege of using the fishing boats or canoes without an adult. This provided a huge amount of freedom for the youngsters, and we all thought it was great and took full advantage of it. All of us have continued this tradition with our children and grandchildren.

By the time the girls, Nilla and Elizabeth, had started school, they had become very interested in horses and riding. This reinvigorated Betsy's interest in the activity, and several things began to happen. The girls were enrolled to get some professional lessons with

Children of all ages in the swimming hole circa 1974

Betsy's friend, Marguerite Ferguson, at her farm near Pontiac, SC. Betsy began taking some lessons herself and before long became a partner with Marguerite running the riding program at Woodcreek. Next, we began to replace some the old horses at the Farm. Over a relatively short period of time, Sir, Hobo, and Lea were acquired as well as a used horse trailer. Some improvements were made in the riding facilities at the Farm. It wasn't long before we had acquired a horse for Nilla (Rita) and Betsy had moved her horse, Lea to Woodcreek as well. Betsy and the girls were riding regularly and all of them were competing some. By the mid 1980s, the idea resurfaced for the first time in 15 years to build our own house and move to the Farm. Betsy actually brought it up, thinking that if we had our own barn and facilities, we could keep our own horses at our house and ride at will. Needless to say, I jumped on it like a chicken on a June bug!

We began trying to decide what we were going to build and most importantly where we were going to build. Once we decided on a site, Betsy and I then negotiated a deal with my parents, and more importantly, with my siblings, whereby we traded some other family assets for roughly 65 acres of our own on which to begin our project.

We selected a site that was at the end of Cate Road across the branch from where our farm manager lived. The first step was to figure out how to access it. We were going to have to

Pond under construction in 1986

63

build a causeway across the creek swamp anyway for our driveway, so we ended up building an eight-acre pond and used the top of the dam as our main road to the house site. We wanted a traditional farmhouse design, and we hired an architect to put together plans that we could take to a builder. Construction began in the summer of 1987. We moved in in June of 1988 and became a full-time farm family.

Pond and house

The years have flown by. The children all graduated from Clemson (much to our pleasure), began lives of their own, and started their own families. Walker married Jules Odom in 1994, and they had three wonderful children, now all pretty much grown themselves: William, born in 1998; Eliza, born in 2000; and John David, 2001. It looks as though all three of them are headed to Clemson as well. William is a senior as of this writing, Eliza is a sophomore, and JD is waiting to hear on his application. It is a blessing to have that common thread with your children and grandchildren. Walker is in the commercial real estate business, and is very active in the management of the Farm. Unfortunately, Walker and Jules's marriage ended after 15 years, but they created a wonderful family of which we are very proud.

Nilla married Sam Hesley in 2004. They have two girls: Catie, born in 2006; and Perry born in 2008. Nilla is a schoolteacher in Bluffton, SC, and Sam is in the construction business. Both girls enjoy riding and volley ball as well as spending time at the Farm with their cousins.

Elizabeth married Pendleton Grove in 2003. They have two boys: John, born 2007; and Walker, born 2009. Elizabeth has spent the last 15 years as a professional horse trainer and riding instructor, but recently moved her horse operation back to the Farm and accepted a position as Upper School Counselor at Heathwood Hall School in Columbia. The common thread here is that that all of the children and grandchildren dearly love the Farm and are regular visitors.

Family at our house circa 2016

One of our family's most satisfying lifetime experiences was the pleasure of having an exchange student from Germany live with us in 1994 and 1995. Kirstin Winkler had grown up in Munich, Germany, and we were given the opportunity to keep her for three weeks during the summer of 1993. She and Elizabeth were the same age, and they bonded immediately upon meeting, and quickly became best friends. Before she left to return home, the girls had concocted the idea for Kirstin to return the next summer and live with us at the Farm and attend Heathwood School for their senior year in high school. Betsy and I had come to love Kirstin as well, so we all went to work to sell the school as well as her parents on the idea.

Nilla was away at Clemson, so Kirstin lived in Nilla's room for the year. She and Nilla also became great friends, so they did not mind sharing her room when she was home. The whole thing was a wonderful experience. We love Kirstin like a daughter. She made lifelong friends while she was here. She learned to drive and obtained a drivers license here. She was here for Walker and Jules wedding, and for the death of my mother. After 25 years the relationship is just as strong. We became friends with her parents, and have visited them a couple of times, and they have come to visit us. Kirstin came back to the Farm to be in Elizabeth's wedding.

Kirstin now lives in Los Angeles and is in the movie business. We see her every few years, and she was here for last Thanksgiving. When she comes, it just seems so natural; we just drop right back into our old relationship, and pick right up where we left off.

Kirstin with Billy, Amos, Lea, and Sophie circa 1995

Charles Hamilton Cate

My older brother Charlie was born September 2, 1938. We all grew up in the house on South Waccamaw and went through Columbia's public school system. All of us went to A.C. Moore Elementary, and Hand Junior High, and Charlie and Betsy went on to high school at Columbia High, whereas I went on to Dreher.

After graduating from the University of South Carolina, Charlie married his high school sweetheart, Audrey Addy, in the summer of 1960. Charlie had just been commissioned an ensign in the Navy through the ROTC program at Carolina, and he and Audrey left immediately after the wedding for active navy duty in California and then ultimately on to Guam, where they would remain for the next two years. I did not see them again until September 1962 before heading off to college myself. I missed them, but they did leave me Charlie's car (1950 Chevrolet station wagon), so I survived just fine.

Once returning from the navy, Charlie began working at Cate-McLaurin Company, and would remain there throughout his career except for the ten years that he left in the 1980s and 1990s to run Associated Industrial Supply, another family-

Picture of the Charles H. Cates

related business. AIS was sold in 1989, and Charlie stayed on with the new owner for two years and then returned to Cate-Mclaurin where we both remained until it was sold to Snider Tire, Inc., a regional commercial tire business in 2000.

After returning to Columbia in 1962, Charlie and Audrey bought their first house on McGregor Drive. Charles Hamilton Cate, Jr. (Charlie) was born in 1963. He was followed Newman Perry Cate (Perry) in 1966 and then Aubrey Franklin Cate (Franklin) in 1976. They all have fine families of their own.

Charlie Jr. married Sue Hardie in 1987, and they have two children, Hardie, born in 1994, and Susannah, born in 1997. Hardie attended Stanford University and is engaged to be married in California to Elizabeth Bernal, and Susannah recently graduated from Davidson.

Perry married Katie Peeples in 1993. Unfortunately their marriage did not last, but they had two fine children, Perry, who earned a degree from Princeton, and Emily, has graduated from Sewanee.

Franklin married Margaret Bothner in 2001, and they live in northern Virginia.

They have three children, David , Elizabeth Grace (EG), and Caroline. The two girls have become great friends with Nilla's girls, Catie and Perry, and David is probably the most enthusiastic Cate hunter and fisherman to come along in several generations, although would probably have some strong competition from William and John David Cate. The jury is still out there, but all of these cousins really enjoy their time together at the Farm.

Sadly, Audrey passed away following a long illness in 2019 as I was writing this chapter. We will all miss her mightily.

Elizabeth Cate Pringle

After finishing Columbia High School in 1958, sister Betsy went off to college at Sweet Briar College near Lexington, Virginia. A side note here is that my father cut some timber at the Farm in order to provide some cash to pay for Betsy's time at Sweet Briar. That was in the days when they moved a portable sawmill to the logging site and milled the logs right there, invariably leaving a large sawdust pile as well as a slab pile on the site. That sawdust pile was immediately named the Sweet Briar Sawdust Pile, and it remained visible for several decades. That whole area of the Farm is known as the Sweet Briar tract to this day.

Betsy has always been very artistic and studied art at Sweetbriar. At any rate, after finishing Sweet Briar, Betsy married John J. (Johnny) Pringle in 1962. Johnny is the older brother to Betsy's lifelong best friend, Eve Pringle Boyd. Eve unfortunately died in 1999. Johnny is extremely well educated, having received an electrical engineering degree from Georgia Tech, a master's in business from Harvard, and a doctorate in business finance from Stanford. Always the engineer, Johnny loves all things technical and is my go-to person whenever I have a need for a higher level of expertise involving electronics.

Johnny spent several years in the business world before he decided that he wanted to be a college-level teacher. He secured a position teaching finance in the graduate school of business at the University of North Carolina. He remained there for the duration of his career, and he and Betsy have made their home in Chapel Hill. Meanwhile, Betsy pursued her career in art and became quite accomplished, selling paintings in galleries across the south. She also became quite expert in wildflowers and native plants, skills that she learned from our mother. She developed a fabulous garden around their 200-year-old house in Chapel Hill. I believe her favorite thing to do is making regular trips to the Farm and checking in on some of the native plants that our mother planted so many years ago.

Betsy and Johnny have four children, John J. Pringle III (Jack), the first-born in 1968. Laura Perry Pringle (Perry) was born in 1971, Joseph LeConte Pringle (Joe) was born in 1973, and Charlie Cate Pringle was born in 1976.

Jack is a lawyer in Columbia. He Married Feilding Zimmerman in 1997. Their marriage did not last, but produced three wonderful children along the way, Jackson, and twins: Lucina and Sawyer.

Perry lives in Florida and is in the commercial art field. Joe married Liza Montgomery in 2003. They have two children: Cate and Wren. They live in northern Virginia.

Charlie married Anne McPherson in 2006. They live in Birmingham and have three children: Betsy, William, and Ellen.

As a family, the Pringles spend a lot of their vacation time at Betsy and Johnny's Lake Toxaway home, but also frequently make trips to the Farm.

One family tradition that persists since the days that Betsy and I began dating, is that for Thanksgiving all of the Cates and the Pringles gather at the Farm House for dinner. It can be quite a crowd, and quite a feast! Last year we had 45 brothers, sisters and cousins, and served wild turkey, domestic, stuffed turkey with all of the trimmings, duck, venison, as well as Betsy Cate's world famous pineapple dish! After several desserts there is a sometimes painful posing for family photographs, followed by a little deer hunting, and a duck hunt the next morning. In the old days, a quail hunt would always have been involved. Sadly, those days appear to be gone. (the quail hunting, that is)

The Pringles at Lake Toxaway

Thanksgiving day circa 1984

Thanksgiving day circa 2004

The Farm

Thanksgiving day 2019

FARM MANAGERS

Since 1950, there have been only three farm managers at Buckeye Farms. I find that to be truly amazing in this day and time, where people change jobs or careers every few years. Think about this for a minute. That is 70 years. Amazing! There is certainly not much money in it. It is hard work! I have always believed that this longevity has happened because of the lifestyle they are allowed to live. They get to live on and have the run of a virtual paradise. Great hunting and fishing right in their front yard, or back yard. Add in that we have always treated our employees fairly and make them feel like family as much as possible. We become friends. In this chapter I will tell you about the three men and their families who have held this position over the last 70 years. I will tell you where they came from and how they came to be here with us.

Farm manager's house at the farm

Before Robert Harris came to work for us in 1950, he was a tenant farmer on our land. He was born about 1920. He came up hard. Robert and his wife Florence lived on and farmed a few acres on a part of the Farm known as Robert's Spring. The house that they lived in was a two-room affair that was uninsulated and had no running water or electricity. Their water came from a spring immediately behind their house. The only evidence that the house was ever there today is a few bricks, household implements, remnants of an old swing, and of course, the spring. The amazing part of Robert's story is that he and Florence had 11 of their 13 children while they were still living in that house. It is a good example of just how primitive things still were in the rural south well into the 1950's.

I do not know how much formal education Robert had. Probably not more than two or three years' worth. He was very intelligent, however. He could read and write fairly legibly, and he was handy and could figure things out better than most people. As a result, he was able to earn a few extra dollars by helping people fix things around the neighborhood. My father got to know him other than just a tenant in this manner and was impressed. So, in 1950, when our manager left us suddenly and moved out of state, Charlie offered the

Roberts Spring today

job to Robert. I doubt if the offer required much deliberation on Robert's part, but at any rate, he accepted and moved his family to a much more substantial house at the end of what is now Cate Road. The older part of the house was probably built in the late nineteenth or early twentieth centuries and is put together quite substantially, being framed with unfinished, full dimension lumber.

Although the house was a huge step up from the house at Roberts Spring, life was still hard. Robert and Florence soon had 13 children in the house to take care of, nine boys and four girls. The house did not have running water inside until Charlie added that later in the 1950s. Also, row crops were still being grown on the Farm. Robert and his children were responsible for looking after the farming operation under Charlie's direction, as well as looking after a fluctuating assortment of cattle, pigs and horses. Robert was quite ingenious at figuring out how to make good use of the resources available to him on the Farm. Of course, he would be, having come up the way he did. He was an excellent woodsman, one of the very best that I have ever known, and he quickly learned to take advantage of the expanding deer herd with an old single shot shotgun. Sometime around 1960, Charlie gave Robert a new Model 870 Remington pump shotgun which he used the rest of his life. Some years later, he told me this story on himself. He had found a big snake in the barn on a floor that he had just installed. Not wanting to damage his new floor, he took a couple of shotgun shells, opened them up and replaced the shot with sugar. Imagine his chagrin when he went back out to dispatch the snake only to "banana peel" the barrel of his new shotgun with the first shot. My father replaced the barrel without comment. Probably a good lesson for my father too, as he never mentioned that story to me. The snake escaped unharmed, pleased with the outcome.

Farming was still very physically hard in those days. Though there was an old Ford tractor on the place, it still required a lot of labor to get things done. Well, Robert had a lot of labor with nine growing boys, and he became quite good at figuring out who could do what and dispatching them efficiently. Some of the boys were a little older than I was, and some a little younger. Since I was frequently on the scene, I often tagged along on projects and participated as I was old enough to actually help. The children and I became friends and have remained so. Some of them still live in the neighborhood, and it always brightens my day when I run into one of them somewhere and we get to visit.

Robert remained in this position for 33 years, retiring in 1983. Over the years he had acquired 12 to 15 acres adjoining the Farm and spent the last 10 years of his employment slowly building his own house in preparation for his retirement. Some of his descendants still live in this settlement.

I have always considered Robert to be one of my most important friends and mentors. He was wise and resourceful in so many ways. With his quiet manner, he was probably not even aware of the many things that he taught me. I have already mentioned that he was an outstanding woodsman, one of the very best that I have ever known. He taught me many woods skills, along with running a chainsaw, and how to properly fell a tree and cut it into firewood. I learned through this process that you were just as tired from running a chainsaw all day as you would have been swinging an axe. The difference is, with a chainsaw, at the end of the day, you have a much bigger pile of wood! But you are just as tired.

One of the most important skills that Robert taught me was how to "still hunt" for deer in the days before that was practiced in South Carolina. In those days, there were not many deer outside of the swamps, and they were only hunted with dogs at that time in the coastal plain. That is the only way we had ever hunted them. Robert never owned a deer rifle, so we had to get very close to have any success with a shotgun. A deer stand would consist of not more than a couple of boards in the fork of a tree situated along a deer trail, or near a pea patch or a persimmon tree. Strangely, deer in those days had not learned that they liked corn. A sophisticated modern deer hunter, with all his fancy, expensive equipment, would likely sneer at our very basic tactics.

Robert also taught me to properly drive a nail, plant a straight row of corn, neatly construct a wire fence, and to take pride in these tasks well done. He wanted these things to be done right, not hurriedly. He didn't want to have to do a project twice and would typically study it for a while before just launching into it. Without even realizing it, he had very good teaching skills, which would come in handy when training his replacement after he retired.

One of our last projects that we did together was to

Charlie and Robert circa 1970

rebuild the bridge that had been blown out for a number of years across the stream above the Pond at the Farm House. Well, we didn't use heavy enough material and it was not properly anchored, so it promptly blew out with first four-inch rain event. I remember Robert standing there, pondering how to put it back so that would not happen again. He said, "Billy, you remember that old wooden bridge that crossed Colonels Creek before Westvaco put in the concrete one?" I nodded. He said, "I know where it is, and I bet that it has got some real good material in it." So, off we went in the farm truck to look at the old bridge that had been lying in the woods for several years. There was indeed some good material in it, particularly the 4 by 10 inch creosote decking boards. Although the original bridge across Colonels Creek was built sometime in the mid 1940s, the creosote material was in pristine condition. It had only been replaced in the late 1970s because logging methods had changed, and the loads of logs became much heavier, as did the machinery used to get the logs out of the woods. The folks at Westvaco were concerned that the foundation of the bridge might not support the increased weight, so they removed it and replaced it with a concrete span. We cut the old bridge apart with chainsaws, crowbars and sledgehammers, and loaded the material in the back of our truck and carried it to our washed-out bridge site. We made a supply run and spent the rest of that day driving 60 penny spikes through those four by ten creosote boards with a five-pound sledge hammer. This task turned both our arm muscles into rubber mush by the end of that afternoon, but I must say, we had a good bridge at the end of the day.

This bridge held solid until the great, historic flood of 2015, when five feet of water blew through there and moved the bridge intact into the woods about 50 feet downstream. At a workday the following summer, we were able to wrestle the bridge back into place using a front-end loader, chains, and some available manpower to guide it. We later anchored it in place with piling and concrete footing. I guess we are good for another twenty years. I have these memories each time that I ride across that bridge.

Robert retired in 1983, and he and Florence moved into the house that he had built on his own land. He continued to help us on a part-time basis for a couple of years. He was also very helpful in breaking in his replacement, Johnny Johnson, teaching him the ropes of managing the cows and horses, as well as the rest of the farm operation, and shepherding the cantankerous old equipment that lived on the Farm at that time.

A lifelong smoker (roll your own Camels), he contracted lung cancer around 1985. He died in 1987. I was asked to speak at his funeral. From my notes, this is more or less what I said:

> First of all, I would like to thank Florence and the rest of the Harrises for the opportunity to make a few farewell remarks about our good friend, Robert.
>
> Everyone has those few special people in their past that have had a real impact on them – helped to shape their life and the person that they were to become. It may have been a favorite uncle or a special friend of the family, but we have all had someone like that. Robert Harris was one of those special people to me. "
>
> I suppose that Robert did not have the advantage of a whole lot of formal education, but he possessed an inner wisdom that he never could have gotten from more schooling. He was extremely intelligent and he knew a lot about a lot of

things. He was always glad to share this knowledge with me. He always seemed to know what to do in a given situation, and I respected his judgement.

I remember as a young man, just back from the army, Robert and I were sitting at the Farm one afternoon, reminiscing about the past and Robert said....'You know Billy, I watched you grow up.' I replied....'No Robert, you helped me grow up!'

Obviously, Robert had lots of friends. It would be hard to know him and not be his friend. He was a complete person – as I have said, he had lots of friends and he had wisdom and good judgement. But he was also a fine family man – husband, father, and grandfather. He was also a devoted churchman. I can see his handywork all over this church building. Of course, he was a valued citizen in this community. Indeed, this would be a very different place without Robert and Florence Harris and all of their fine children and grandchildren.

I hope that you can see that Robert Harris occupied a very special place in my life. I am thankful to have been his friend. Amen.

When Robert was getting ready to retire in 1983, my father, Charlie, was really beginning to worry about how to replace him. He was visualizing a family like the Harrises that had children that would provide a ready source of farm labor. Things had really changed from the 1950s and 60s, and I had a different view of what we were going to need. By then I was making most of the management decisions at the Farm and asked my father if I could find Robert's replacement.

Robert in early 1980s

79

Life in the 80s was a whole lot more complicated than it had been in earlier decades, and it was certainly way more expensive to raise a family. For that reason, I did not think it wise to have a growing family in our employ and living in our house. Their problems would become our problems. I felt that hiring someone whose children were grown but young enough to still be able to do the work was what we needed. Furthermore, I felt that we had more than just a job here, and that we had a lifestyle to sell that I felt would appeal to a broad range of people. It turns out that my hunch was correct. I ran a simple classified ad in the newspaper (people still read the classifieds back then), stressing the lifestyle benefits such as a house provided, available hunting and fishing, and the run of a 1200-acre farm. I did ask that they have some knowledge of equipment and be somewhat proficient at fixing things. I asked that they reply in writing to a blind post office box. The mail started coming in almost immediately. If memory serves, I received about forty written responses, which bolstered my belief that we were on the right track. Some of the candidates were under qualified and some were overqualified. I actually interviewed about six, I think.

We settled on the perfect fit for us, I think. Johnny Johnson and his wife Trudy moved to the Farm right after Robert and Florence moved out in August of 1983. The house

Johnny and me at a cattlemen meeting circa mid 1980s

needed some work and a few upgrades, and Johnny made some suggestions and volunteered to do some the work himself. I told him that we would provide materials for any project that he could do himself.

Johnny had grown up on a farm in North Dakota, and Trudy grew up on one in Missouri. As soon as Johnny was old enough, he left the farm and joined the army. Army life suited him, and he made a career of it, retiring as a senior NCO. He and Trudy had five fine children, all of whom were grown by the time they moved here. He was 49 years old at the time, had his army retirement and all of the benefits. Over the years he had come to realize that he missed farm life and longed to settle back down on a farm. Our job represented the perfect opportunity for him and for us! Johnny took right to it, and with Robert working with him a couple of days a week, he learned the ropes quickly. He was especially good with animals, but I think he really enjoyed all phases of farm life and made it his mission to produce as much of their own food as possible. He did not waste anything! When he would kill a deer, he would waste not one part of it! He even had a recipe for pickled deer heart. It was quite good I might add.

Johnny had a tendency to leave tools around wherever he might be working on something. Robert did too, for that matter. In Johnny's case, however, he had a lot of his own tools, and he was just as likely to lose his own as mine. I accused them both at various times of running a tool farm. Every time that we would plow a field, we would turn up at least one of our old tools. This still happens fairly often I might add while plowing. The sight of the old tool usually stirs a memory or so.

Johnny was also a little accident-prone. That's not my imagination, by the way. When somebody seems accident prone, it is a pretty good bet that they are. One particular day in Johnny's time at the Farm stands out. His son was here visiting for a while, and Johnny solicited Vernon's help in trimming up the road on the way into the house. He got Vernon to run him and the chainsaw up in the bucket of the front-end loader so that he could reach a hard to get at limb with the saw. Well, the chainsaw got away from him and inflicted a nasty gash in his calf. Trudy carried him to the emergency room at Moncrief Army Hospital at Fort Jackson, where they spent the rest of the day getting the leg stitched up. When Trudy was driving them home that night, someone ran into the back of the truck throwing Johnny's head back into the rear window, breaking the glass and slicing his scalp. Back to Moncrief Hospital they go, where they find the same army doc on duty in the emergency room. "Not you again!" he said as they came through the door, bleeding from the other end this time.

Once Johnny approached 65, I began to wonder just how long he might want to do the kind of work that the job sometimes required. He assured me that he wasn't ready to stop, and that he would give me plenty of notice when he was ready. He was good to his word on that, and later told me that he intended to work until August 2003, the twentieth anniversary of his start date at the Farm. He was 69 at the time and still in perfect health. He continued to help us on an as needed basis for several years and still occasionally comes deer hunting with us. He is now 85 and still in remarkably good shape. Sadly, Trudy passed away a few years ago following a long illness.

We had been gradually reducing our cattle herd over the last few years of Johnny's stay here and sold the last few just before his retirement. I also leased out the hay field, with the plan to just put up enough square bale hay to feed the horses through the winter, usually 400 to 600 bales depending on how many horses we were keeping at the time. The only farming that we were doing by then was for wildlife such as duck ponds and game patches for deer and turkeys. Accordingly, I felt that we no longer needed full-time help. Clearly, we needed someone reliable living in that house to help look out for things and to help with projects as they came up.

I envisioned a part-time person who had a full-time job with benefits that our set up would appeal to. Thinking that would appeal to someone working at the South Carolina Department of Natural Resources (DNR) or the South Carolina Forestry Commission, I put the word out to some of my contacts at both agencies. Remember, that we had already shown that our position provided some very appealing perks to people who loved the out-of-doors, not to mention the great hunting and fishing at your fingertips.

My old friend Drew Robb, who worked in Fisheries at DNR, suggested that I might want to talk with his friend and co-worker Treye Byars. After Drew told me about him, I agreed, and he arranged a meeting. I did not know Treye but knew of him. He was a lifelong Eastover boy, having grown up in the area, and his family actually went to the same church that we did, Saint Johns Congaree. I did know his mother and his brother. Treye was recently divorced and was co-parenting his seven-year-old daughter, Taylor.

Treye came to live and work here in August of 2003 and is here to this day. At the time when he first came, he was working for DNR as a technician in the

Treye and Taylor

Fisheries Section at the Wateree office right down the road from his house, which was very convenient for all concerned. Treye and Taylor fit right in with our routine here, and adapted quite well to the lifestyle. Taylor basically grew up on the Farm. She went to school in Sumter, graduated from Clemson University, and is working as a wildlife biologist for a waterfowl center in the Central Valley in California.

Treye transferred from Fisheries to Law Enforcement six to eight years ago and has been working as a game warden since then. While it is great having a law enforcement officer on the Farm, Treye doesn't have nearly as much control over his time as he did when he was in Fisheries. This complicates our scheduling farm projects to some degree, especially when it requires more than one person, and it becomes necessary for us to work on a project together. We make it work however, and it has been a great fit for both of us. Treye became engaged to his longtime girlfriend, Gina. We like her very much, and so does his mother!

Over the years we have adapted our job to suit the needs of the Farm as times changed. I had thought that when we

Treye with his dad Wick when receiving Officer of the Year award

decided to go the part-time route, that we would likely be changing managers every few years. It obviously has not worked out that way, and it has reinforced my view that our position offers so much more than just a job. It provides a lifestyle that most of our potential managers would have a hard time creating on their own.

Dogs

Anyone who knows us, knows that we are dog lovers of the highest order. I have always had a dog and really cannot imagine life without one. In an earlier time, we always had hunting dogs, and many of them were not considered family pets. Of course, some were the dearest of family pets, but my plan here is to devote this chapter to the 13 dogs that Betsy and I have had over the course of our marriage that were not just pets but were complete members of the family and were loved and doted on accordingly.

Our lifelong friend Cal McMeekin once said, "Damn Cate, when I come back in my next life, I want to come back as Billy Cate's dog." I replied, "Hell Slick, when I come back in my next life, I want to come back as Billy Cate's dog!" There is no question, they have had it good! Dogs create the finest kind of friendship, with unconditional love and loyalty. They do not care if you have got any money or not, what you look like, or what your religion is. They will love you even if you do not deserve it. We have all seen people with their dogs and wondered why they even had a dog in the first place, they were so indifferent toward it. Even then the dog remains steadfastly loyal.

Long before I ever had the idea to write a book, I had wondered how to memorialize the really special dogs that we had owned. I realized that after we were gone, nobody would even know they had ever existed. Somehow, that just did not seem right to me, that a friend as special as Amos, or Bizzy, or Dottie could just be, I don't know, poof – and gone, with nobody to ever think of them again. Along about the time when I first started thinking about this, I was carving walking sticks out of persimmon wood. I carved one especially for our 13 dogs listing their names and the years of their lives on it. That way, as long as one of our descendants kept the stick it would serve as a memorial to these special friends.

Walking stick memorializing our dogs

When Betsy and I were first married in 1966, I had a wonderful 2-year-old Labrador Retriever named Amos. Amos was really the second Amos, as my family had another Lab of that name when I was growing up. For my purposes here, we will stick to the ones that Betsy and I have had. He was amazingly smart, and an exceptional hunting dog, and I was really proud of him. It was heartbreaking to leave him when we reported to army duty in El Paso, Texas, not knowing when we would see him again. After about two months, we were both having serious dog withdrawals. By then, we had figured out that we were going to be there for a while. "Let's get a dog," we said, and agreed that we wanted a beagle puppy. It would make a great pet and could help me hunt deer when we got back to South Carolina. After studying the dog ads, we found a beautiful litter of puppies and came home with Rebel, an adorable tri-colored beagle pup with big brown eyes that could stare right through you.

We flew back to Columbia for two weeks Christmas leave and took Rebel with us. We had driven Betsy's car to El Paso and had left mine at Betsy's parents' house for her sister Anne to drive with the plan to drive it to back to Texas whenever we came home. So, when we drove my car back on New Year's Eve, 1966, Amos accompanied us, making our little family complete, at least for now.

The dogs were certainly at the center of our lives as we rode out our army time. Amos especially went just about everywhere with me when I was off duty. He got a tremendous amount of retriever work, as I got in a lot of duck and dove hunting while stationed at Fort Bliss. Bliss is a gigantic army base covering several hundred thousand acres in west Texas and southern New Mexico. I had access to most of it and quickly learned that if you could find water, you could find doves, and lots of them! And large quantities of ducks when they were migrating through on their way to Mexico and Central America. All you had to do was find the water.

After getting off active duty and returning to Columbia, and after Walker was born, we were spending a week at the Farm in July of 1969, and Amos inexplicably wandered off and stayed gone all night. I found him dead on the highway the next morning, as he had been struck by a car. I was devastated. It was my first experience losing a dog that I was so close to. I have since come to realize why losing a dog is so hard. In our society, you don't get the time to

Amos and Rebel 1968

properly grieve the loss of a pet. Nor do you have the support group to help you cope. You are expected to get on with your life, and you are expected to do so with a big hole in your heart. My mother, Nilla, gave me some sound advice at this time when she knew I was hurting. "The best way to get over the loss of a dog that you love, is to get another dog!"

Rebel was as broken up as Betsy and I were. He just moped around and would barely eat for several weeks. As luck would have it, we learned of a litter of labs with the same bloodlines as Amos that winter and was able to secure a male puppy in early 1970 and named him Judge. Life was whole again.

Judge and Rebel both led full lives, hanging out with the Cate children and making regular trips to the Farm. Judge is the only dog that we had that lived with us in each of our first three houses that we owned in Columbia. He was quiet and lovable and a very good duck retriever, not overly aggressive, but very systematic and

Judge and Walker circa 1970

methodical with a highly tuned nose. He died of old age at fourteen in 1983.

Rebel contracted cancer at age nine and died in early 1975. Our friend Bill Jennings, who lived in Charlotte at the time, just happened to have a litter of beagle puppies at the time and offered one to us. Next trip to Columbia he delivered Jenny, a sweet and beautiful tri-color female, who became an instant family favorite. She was also a very talented deer hound and was much acclaimed by my many deer hunting buddies at the time.

Our second Amos came from our old family line of Labradors - as did the first Amos and Judge. We called it the Queenie line, as Queenie was the first lab from that line that our family knew of, and she came to my parents as a pup from some family friends. The Queenie line produced some wonderful dogs for a lot of different people. They all were very handsome dogs, relatively small at 65 pounds or so, and had very similar

Jenny on a romp

Amos, Billy, and Walker circa 1985

personality traits. At any rate, Amos was born in 1984. I think that we got him that summer in June. I knew from day one that he was going to be a major star. He had all of the best qualities of retriever instincts. I was doing quite a bit of duck hunting in those days, and he went right to work. As I recall, he was six months old on his first duck hunt, and he performed like an

Amos II, Elizabeth, Nilla, and Billy on new dam circa 1987

eight-year veteran. I think that he flawlessly retrieved six ducks on that first hunt. Not only that, he behaved perfectly in the blind.

Amos was the most polished retriever I ever owned. Not only did he have all of the natural instincts, he got a lot of hands-on groundwork. He was worked every day after my work. It was something that we both looked forward to. I was in a very pressure-packed, stressful job in those days, and it was how I would use that time to unwind at the end of the day. I would come home, get a cold beer, get Amos, and go retrieve for 15 to 30 minutes. It was an everyday ritual that we did together for as long as he was with us, at least until he became infirm in his last year. He died at age twelve in 1996.

Sophie showed up on our back steps Thanksgiving morning 1988. She appeared to be about six months old and most likely a cross between a golden retriever and a cocker spaniel. She looked like a miniature golden with the same gentle disposition and those soft brown eyes. We had no idea where she came from. She had just wandered up, somehow picking out our house from all the others on Cate Road. Of course, the girls were all over her. When my mother, Nilla, arrived for Thanksgiving, she too was all over her. Of course,

Sophie as an older dog

she was cute. When people started leaving after lunch, Sophie
(They had already named her) had disappeared. I was sort of
relieved and hoping that she had just gone back where she
had come from as we already had two dogs, Amos and Jenny.
No such luck, as when my mother (The children called her
GrandNilla) was driving out, she saw Sophie out on the road
by the mailboxes. Naturally, she picked her up, turned around,
and brought her right back to the house. "That dog is meant to
be here!" she said. All debate on the subject was over. Sophie
was our dog!

Several weeks later I was up at Bunky's store one night
and noticed a sign on the wall that said someone had lost and
was looking for a sweet golden retriever cross. I knew it had to
be Sophie. I dreaded telling the girls, and when I told them at
supper, they both dissolved in tears. Figuring I might as well
get it over with, I called the number after supper, and guess
what? It wasn't Sophie! The girls were beside themselves. I
guess Sophie was relieved too, with all the hugs and kisses she
was getting. She had struck pay dirt!

Sophie quickly became Elizabeth's dog, and when she
moved out in 2001 or so, Sophie went with her. She lived a
long life and was much loved. She died at age 16 in 2004 and is
buried with the other family dogs and horses at what is known
as Sir's Ridge.

Our first Jack Russell terrier, Izzy, came along in 1991.
JR's are kind of a "horse thing" and are very popular around
riding facilities. Betsy and both girls were riding a lot at
that time. Elizabeth was taking it quite seriously and riding
regularly with Ron Danta, a trainer in Camden. He had a
litter of Jack Russell puppies and started working on Betsy to
take one. Of course, the girls were working on her too. She
convinced me that we could handle another dog. At that time,
we had Amos and Sophie. Izzy was an instant hit and won
me over quickly. She was mostly a house dog and was a very
easy keeper. In fact, she was such an easy keeper, when she was
about two, Ron suggested that we breed her to his favorite male
dog, Gadget.

Izzy's litter was born just after New Years, 1993. The birth
was ten days early, which is extremely early for a dog. This is
where the story becomes really interesting and worth retelling.
Betsy realized quickly that something was wrong. She delivered
a couple of puppies in the kitchen, but they were really tiny

Izzy with Betsy and riding students

and one was born dead. They were way too tiny and did not appear to be completely developed. She bundled up Izzy and the puppies and went to town to the veterinarian, where they spent the rest of the day, operating and delivering the rest of the puppies. In total, there were eight delivered, and two were dead, leaving six very immature pups that needed their mother very badly. Izzy and the pups came home that night and Izzy was doing her best in her condition to take care of them. Well, the next day (Sunday afternoon), something was clearly wrong with Izzy. She was listless and appeared to be going in to shock. Betsy rushed her to the emergency vet where it was determined she had a severe infection from the dead puppies staying inside of her for too long and had essentially poisoned her. The doctor recommended an emergency hysterectomy, stating that was her only chance to survive, but that she might not. She didn't. We were heartbroken, but quickly realized that we didn't have time to be because we had 6 tiny, less than two-day old premature pups in our kitchen, that were going to need a lot of help to have any chance of survival.

The pups started dying one at a time, and by the end of the second day, we were down to one. Nilla was back at Clemson, but Elizabeth was still in high school. She, Betsy and

I made a commitment to save that puppy. You have to realize what we were dealing with. We had a 4-day old puppy that had been born 10 days premature, whose mother had died the next day. He literally was not as large as a very small mouse. The first step was for Betsy to have a serious conversation with the vet about what steps we should take if we were to have a chance at success. He asked if the puppies had nursed at all. Betsy told him that they had nursed during that first 24 hours until Izzy went into shock. He said that if he had indeed nursed for several hours, he would have received enough of his mother's colostrum to give him the anti-bodies he would need to have a decent chance at surviving. He gave us a very strict regimen to follow for several weeks, with the first two being the most critical. Elizabeth, Betsy and I agreed to divide shifts in taking care of him. Betsy's friend, Peggy Heard, from Montgomery, Alabama, visited during this time and gladly helped with the duty.

By then we had decided to name him Bizzy, in honor of Izzy. Bizzy was living in a box in the kitchen with a light on him to keep him warm. Every three hours around the clock he had to be given formula with an eye dropper. We would use warm, damp cotton to wipe his little bottom to stimulate a bowel movement, emulating his mother licking him. Betsy started getting little stuffed animals about his size to put in the box with him to help him feel like he had siblings in the box with him. As he started to grow, Betsy would increase the size of the animals to approximate Bizzy's size. He never saw another dog until he was about eight weeks old. For the rest of his life (17.5 years) Bizzy would

Bizzy at approximately one year old circa 1994

have an affinity for stuffed animals and always had several to carry around and snuggle with. He developed a very unusual character trait that I am convinced came from the way he came into the world. We called it "trancing", but he would take one of his favorite animals, hold it in his mouth, wrap his front legs around it, lie down on his belly, and zone out with his eyes open, truly going into a trance. You could wave your hands in front of his face and get no effect. It might last as long as five to ten minutes, and he was truly someplace else while in his trance. I never saw him levitate, but we always expected him to.

Because of his unusual and abnormal early life, Bizzy will always hold a special place in our hearts. He became a constant companion and made a lot of friends with his highly unusual personality. As a bonus, he was a great hunting dog. He had a superior nose and was highly praised for his ability to trail a wounded deer. He will always be one of the special ones. After he died in 2010 of old age at 17.5 years old, Elizabeth gave me the painting below for my next birthday that she commissioned

Bizzy in a trance

Meredith Paysinger to do for her of Bizzy. I consider it a treasure!

Painting of Bizzy

Bizzy was such a complete success as a family dog, that after a couple of years, Betsy and I thought that we would like to perpetuate his family line. Of course, the first step was to find him a wife. Betsy did the research and in early 1994, found a litter she liked in Aiken and came home with Blossom, a six or seven week-old tri-color female. She adapted to life on the Farm. Like Bizzy, she lived in the house, but outside she was a born hunter. She was extremely fast and agile and could jump amazingly high. She would chase anything, but her favorites were squirrels and moles. If she smelled a mole in the ground, she would start digging. She was not to be denied. She might dig a 50-foot trench across the yard until she came up with the mole, which she would instantly kill and immediately abandon. Good riddance on the mole, but very hard on the lawn.

Blossom reclining in bed

I personally saw her catch and kill two squirrels and saw the results of her efforts on numerous other times when she would deliver her trophy to the back steps and deposit it there. Her hunting technique was that she would park herself under a tree with a squirrel in it and just sit motionless, sometimes for several hours. Sometimes she could entice the squirrel into working its way down the tree a bit at a time trying to tease Blossom. She would remain motionless as the squirrel worked its way closer and closer. The fatal mistake would come when the squirrel did not realize how high Blossom could jump.

She would spring off the ground with an incredible leap, take several steps up the side of the tree before the squirrel could react and bank off the tree with the surprised squirrel in her teeth, shaking her head violently on the way down. The squirrel would be stone dead by the time she landed.

Bizzy and Blossom had two litters together. The second one was born in 1999 and there were only two puppies. We gave the female to Johnny Johnson, our farm manager, and we kept the male, naming him Weston. Weston was a great dog with a wonderful disposition, but unfortunately, he spent most of his life in the shadow of his amazing parents. We

Weston on patrol

kept telling him, "One day Weston, you are going to get to be Number One Dog!"

Blossom and Weston did quite a lot hunting together and would run off together and sometimes stay gone for several hours. Their mole trenches could be quite impressive! One time at our mountain house, they ran off and burrowed into a skunk's den and then really paid the price. We paid the price too! They came back completely covered with black mud and skunk stink. We never did think we would get them clean and rid of the smell. It was weeks before the smell completely left them!

The hunting was eventually Blossom's downfall. When she got after something, she could not leave it alone. In the spring of 2005, she and Weston went off on one of their great hunts. They were gone for several hours and Betsy started looking for them, as I was not at home. Weston finally came back without his momma. Betsy then went back in the direction he had come from and found her down by the Duck Pond with her head caught in an irrigation pipe. She was dead. Our guess is the probably chased a lizard or a mouse into the pipe and got her head stuck in the process of trying to get to it. We never figured out whether she suffocated or broke her neck while trying to escape. It was very traumatic. I sadly buried her at "Sir's Ridge".

In early 2010 Betsy and I went to Aiken and acquired a 12-week-old Jack Russell who we named Dottie. We selected her from a huge selection of puppies because of her good looks and particularly for her quiet and affectionate disposition, which is what we always looked for in our dogs. We had also acquired her to be the surrogate mother for Bizzy's puppies. You see, about four years before, we had had a veterinarian collect a couple of straws of Bizzy's semen and had them frozen in his clinic in Alabama. Bizzy was thirteen at the time. Sounds crazy, right? Well the plan was, after he had passed away, we were to break old Biz out of the freezer and artificially inseminate Dottie (clinically of course), and voila', Bizzy, the ultimate dog is recreated! Well, it didn't work. When Dottie was almost two, we took her to the clinic in Alabama for a week to perform the insemination, but it just didn't take. All is well that ends well, however, and Dottie has turned out to be the ultimate dog.

Ever since we got her, Dottie has been my constant companion. She and Bizzy are so much alike in looks and manner, I frequently call her Bizzy by mistake. She goes just about everywhere with me. I was working at the Congaree

Dottie on deer stand

Land Trust at that time, and we had a dog friendly office, so she went with me to the office every day. She pretty quickly became the "Company Dog". I wish that I had discovered that trick when I was working at Cate-McLaurin. It is such a stress reliever in the middle of a very hectic day, to just go outside with your dog and walk around the neighborhood. I also wish I had known that trick when I was a young guy and looking for girls. It amazing how many pretty girls will stop you in Five Points to visit with your dog!

Dottie has a very endearing trait, that kind of reminds me of Bizzy's "trancing". She loves to watch television, especially animal shows. She can be sound asleep, and I can say, "Dottie, you better come look!" She will jump up and run to the TV, and will watch intently until something else comes on.

Dottie watching her animal shows

Weston contracted cancer at age 12 and died in 2012. He is buried under a pile of stones next to Bizzy and Blossom on "Sir's Ridge". For the next couple of years, we operated as a one-dog family for the first time and were beginning to think we were going to stay that way.

Well, that did not happen. Our friend Peggy Heard, who had given us the idea to save some of Bizzy's semen several years ago, called Betsy and said that she had a rescue project for her. A friend of hers had a really cute long-haired Jack Russell that she couldn't keep. She just had too many dogs. She sent pictures, and he really was cute. He was 15 months old at the time. He also had come from the same breeder that Dottie had come from. Betsy told me that she thought that we could keep another dog, especially since we had always had at least two. Betsy was staying at our mountain house at that time, and Peggy said she would come for a visit and bring him to us. We decided to name him Weston, in honor of old Weston, who never got to be "Number One Dog." The deal was set.

Weston relaxing

No question about it, Weston is really cute, but when he came in as a rescue project from Alabama, he was an emotional wreck. So much so that Peggy said that she started to turn around a couple of times and take him back to the girl she had gotten him from. He was afraid of everything and everyone. He particularly had an issue with men. He would not let you get your hands on him, even to touch him. So, for the first couple of weeks that we had him, we left a short leash attached to his collar. If you were gentle and patient, you could usually get within range of the end of the leash. Once you got your hands on the leash, he would calm down, and he would act fairly normal as long as he was leashed. He discovered after a couple of days, that he really liked to be in Betsy's lap, and he became perfectly relaxed there. That remains his favorite spot, and it is not unusual for him to spend a couple of hours a day there.

Well, we were patient and worked with him, and he gradually became more or less normal and has become a very satisfactory pet, especially when he is with just Betsy and me

Dottie and Weston patrolling the farm

and Dottie. In fact, he and Dottie have always gotten along great. I think dogs are happier if they live with another dog. It allows them to sometimes just be a dog. Weston is still a little quirky and is very protective of his people, particularly Betsy. He barks at all strangers (not all bad) and most men. If he is riding in the cab of my truck, and somebody that he doesn't know well reaches inside the cab for any reason, he will likely do more than just bark. His teeth are very sharp!

We have had a lot of great, wonderful dogs, and the ones described in this chapter are all great and wonderful, and we have loved them dearly. I have been frequently asked," Do you have a favorite?" I have thought about that a lot over the years, and I do have a group of favorites. At the time that I had them, I would have said that "This is the best dog I have ever owned!" So, I guess it's kind of era-related, but this is my list of who I consider the best of the best!

The Best of the Best
Amos 1964 - 1969
Amos 1984 – 1996
Bizzy 1993 – 2010
*Dottie 2009 - 2021

I guess it's pretty obvious that dogs have been a big part of our family and of our lives, particularly before the children, and after the children had grown up and left. I have a saying that I especially like that I will close this chapter with.

"Children grow up too fast, and dogs don't live long enough"

*See chapter on randon thoughts.

The Conservation Easement

In 2001 we placed a conservation easement on our family's 1250 acre farm. At that time, conservation easements were still relatively new in South Carolina, and not many people knew a whole lot about them, including us. We had to go to school on the process before we could even begin to decide if it was something that we really wanted to do. This chapter deals with that thought process, and describes how it has worked out for us. Hopefully it might give readers an idea how an easement might be useful on their own land.

I have the good fortune to live on and manage our family's 1200-acre farm near the Wateree River in the COWASEE Basin. It is owned presently by myself, my brother, and my sister, and it is set up as an LLC. It has been in my family since the mid-1940s. My parents dearly loved this land, and I have always considered it a family legacy. We all have grown children, and now grandchildren, and had for many years worried about the difficulty subsequent generations were going to have deciding the highest and best use of the land and how to manage it going forward.

The notion of a conservation easement on our farm first formed around 1995 and it then became an evolutionary process. We began to seriously consider placing an easement on the Farm in 2000 and completed it in late 2001. Some of the things that we considered were the effect on future generations, what were our long-term goals for our land, what rights were we willing to give up, and which rights that we wished to retain. Two things that we knew we wanted was to not have a large up-front, out-of-pocket cost, and that we did not want our tax deduction for the easement to be challenged by the

Internal Revenue Service. Or, if it was challenged, that our numbers would hold up under scrutiny.

All three of us came to realize about this time that none of us ever wanted to see our property developed. We discussed this aspect with all of our children, and they all felt really good about the easement concept as well, since none of them wanted any development taking place on the land either. Once we all realized that everyone felt the same way about this, the thought process became quite easy from that point on. My friend and former lawyer, John McLeod, had recently gone to work for

Formerly endangered Wood Storks at the Farm by Ron Ahle

the Congaree Land Trust. I had always been very comfortable with John and knew that we could count on him to do an excellent job for us, so we cast our lot with Congaree to put our easement together. That led to a whole new adventure for me, as I have been involved with Congaree Land Trust in one capacity or another for the last two decades.

In our easement, we gave up our development and subdivision rights, but we retained all of our agricultural, forestry, and recreational rights, requiring only that we follow best management practices. In essence, the conservation easement required us to keep doing what we had always done with our land. The easement is perpetual so any future owner would be bound by its terms. Once we made the decision to move forward, we never gave a second thought as to whether we were doing the right thing for our family and for our land.

A very important point, that did not occur to us until we were well along in the process, is that by placing a conservation easement on our farm, we diffused the inevitable future family feud over what to do with the land. A future generation can sell it, if they need to or want to, subject to the terms of the easement of course, but they will not be able to argue over whether to develop it or not.

I have not talked about the financial aspect of a conservation easement. The tax benefits can be considerable, and they have been very meaningful to my family. That was not the overriding criteria for us, however. First and foremost, we were interested in protecting the land and keeping it in traditional land uses such as forestry or agriculture. Since this time, I have been involved in a lot of conservation easements, and I have found that the vast majority of landowners are more interested in the land protection side of the equation as opposed to the financial side. This is particularly true with multigenerational family-owned land. What I do think is that a conservation easement is a great way to have your cake and still eat some of it too. There simply are not many of those kinds of deals out there. I have come to think of a conservation easement as exercising the "ultimate property right". I get to decide how my land is going to be managed long after I'm gone, no matter who owns it! I think that is pretty cool. I am quite sure that my parents would think it was pretty cool too!

I will not try to tell you that a conservation easement is for everybody or for every piece of land, but if it fits, it is a very painless way to protect special places or important family land forever.

COWASEE Basin

The COWASEE Basin Task Force was created in 2005 in order to establish a major focus area along the Congaree, Wateree, and Santee Rivers that is now known as the COWASEE Basin. COWASEE is an acronym for the three rivers that comprise the basin area - Congaree, Wateree, Santee. The task force is a unique partnership between various conservation organizations and a group of interested landowners. The members of the task force are shown below.

Congaree Land Trust
Conservation Fund
Ducks Unlimited
Audubon South Carolina
The Nature Conservancy
Friends of Congaree Swamp
Natural Resources Conservation Service
Richland County Conservation Commission
SC Department of Natural Resources
Sumter County Conservation District
US Fish and Wildlife Service
Landowners: Roy Belser, Billy Cate, John Cely, Angus Lafaye, Brook Moore, Hugh Ryan, Hank Stallworth, Dick Watkins, Bob Perry, Buddy Baker

The COWASEE Basin Focus Area is patterned after the highly successful ACE Basin (Ashepoo, Combahee, Edisto) in the Lowcountry. The COWASEE focus area includes approximately 315,000 acres with largest amount being in Richland and Sumter Counties but also includes large blocks in Kershaw, Lexington, and Calhoun Counties (see map). It is anchored by the beautiful and fascinating Congaree

National Park in Richland County. Congaree National Park is about 27,000 acres in size and is the only national park in South Carolina. It is also the largest acreage of old growth bottomland hardwood in North America. The park contains 6 national champion trees as well as 24 state champions.

COWASEE is also the location of Poinsett State Park, one of South Carolina's nicest state parks, as well as Manchester State Forest, Congaree Bluffs Heritage Preserve, and the incredibly beautiful Sparkleberry Swamp. Additionally, the newly acquired 4000-acre Wateree Heritage Preserve has been added to this list of scenic and accessible sites. A beautiful section of the Palmetto Trail treks through COWASEE.

COWASEE Basin also incldes working farms and forests.
Congaree Land Trust photo

COWASEE is an area of both cultural and historical significance, beginning with the ancient Native American cultures, already noted. Hernando De Soto and his army of conquistadors moved through COWASEE in 1540 in search of Indian gold on his well-documented exploration of the southeast providing the first European contact with the natives of COWASEE. English explorer John Lawson provided vivid descriptions of what COWASEE looked like when first seen by Europeans. During the Revolutionary War, significant

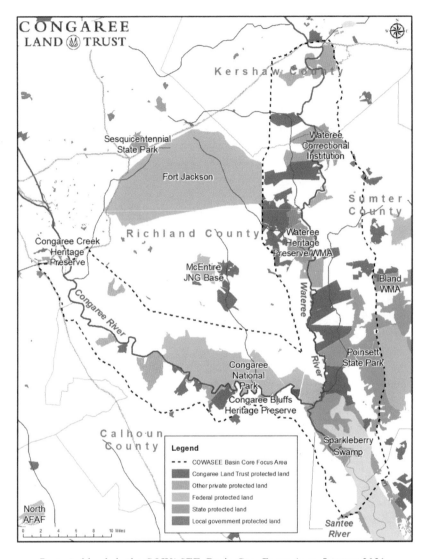

CONGAREE
LAND TRUST

Kershaw County

Sesquicentennial
State Park

Fort Jackson

Wateree
Correctional
Institution

Sumter
County

Congaree Creek
Heritage
Preserve

Richland County

Wateree
Heritage
Preserve/WMA

McEntire
JNG Base

Bland
WMA

Congaree River

Wateree

River

Poinsett
State Park

Congaree
National
Park

Congaree Bluffs
Heritage Preserve

Calhoun
County

Legend

- - - COWASEE Basin Core Focus Area

Congaree Land Trust protected land

Other private protected land

Federal protected land

State protected land

Local government protected land

Sparkleberry
Swamp

North
AFAF

0 2 4 6 8 10 Miles

Santee
River

Protected lands in the COWASEE Basin Core Focus Area, January 2021

battles were fought in the COWASEE Basin area involving
legendary leaders General Cornwallis for the British, and
Generals Nathaniel Greene, Thomas Sumter, and Francis
Marion for the Colonials. During the American Civil War,
numerous skirmishes were fought in COWASEE as what
was left of the ragtag rebel army tried to slow the Union war
machine led by General William T. Sherman in early 1865.
Several notable plantation houses survive today in COWASEE.
They are all very different in appearance but beautifully

107

Broadwater Creek by Jim Kelly

maintained. They are Kensington, Mulberry, Milford, and the Borough House.

About half of the acreage in the COWASEE Basin is river swamp bottomland, while the balance is mixed hardwood and pine woodlands or farmland. Several things make this area unique. First and foremost, it is largely unspoiled. One reason for this is that most of the land in these river basins is held in large tracts from several hundred to several thousand acres each. Many of these tracts have been owned by the same families for generations. Landowners are encouraged to protect their land through the use of voluntary conservation easements.

One of the things that is amazing to me is how few people in the highly populated midlands realize the truly special places and spectacular scenery that is right under their nose. It is always surprising to meet so many local people that have never been to Congaree National Park (the only national park in South Carolina), or who think you have to go to Florida to capture a setting like the incomparable Sparkleberry Swamp.

As a local landowner, my memories of the COWASEE Basin span nearly 75 years. It is remarkable to note that the beautiful landscape seen today is almost exactly the way it was when I first remember it as a little boy. That is really saying

Pine Island Creek in Sparkleberry Swamp by John Cely

something when you realize that the closest entry point to the COWASEE Basin is less than five miles from downtown Columbia and the furthermost point is only 40 miles from the South Carolina State House.

My good friend John Cely wrote a beautiful book, *COWASEE Basin: The Green Heart of South Carolina*, perfectly describing the area where I have lived, worked, hunted and fished, and explored my entire lifetime. John's book contains stunning photography and the fascinating history of the COWASEE Basin. It is still available at the Congaree Land Trust and various retail outlets.

I am pleased to report that at this writing, much progress has been made to protect the Basin's iconic red river bottomland. To date, approximately fifty percent of the 315,000 acres is protected through public or private conservation easements.

Natural Catastrophes

Over the last 30 years or so The Farm has suffered through three catastrophic natural disasters. Oh yes, we have had the periodic winter ice storm that have been terribly annoying and have required short term cleanup inconveniences, army worm infestations in crops, and other nuisance events that make you lie awake at night. But the three disasters mentioned in this chapter were much more long term in nature and altered the way that we manage our forest for years to come. The events that I refer to are Hurricane Hugo in 1989, the Great Flood in 2015, which are well known and documented, and thirdly, the ips beetle outbreak in five counties in South Carolina in 2019. The beetle problem was not well known because it was not widespread, and it impacted far fewer people than the other two, but It created quite a problem at Buckeye Farms, and frankly created similar future timber management problems as did the other two.

Hurricane Hugo

Hurricane Hugo was a horrific event in South Carolina, and it was up close and personal at The Farm. The hurricane hit the Farm in the early morning hours of Friday, September 22, 1989. We were expecting hurricane force winds, but nothing like what occurred. Walker was off at Clemson, and Betsy and I were home with Nilla and Elizabeth and Nilla's good friend Liz Barron and Elizabeth's good friend, Elizabeth Wolfe. The power had gone off about nine o'clock, so we went to bed early, expecting the main storm about daylight the next morning.

We had debated at feeding time whether to leave the horses in the barn or turn them out, finally deciding to turn them out, thinking that that if it got really bad overnight, they would be safer and less frantic outside. Before turning in, I had let the dogs, Amos and Jenny (now 14 years old) out to do their business. Amos came right back and I let him in, but Jenny, being a beagle, picked that time to wander off. I called for a while, but it was raining hard, and the wind was blowing in gusts. I gave up and went to bed. At least it was warm.

About two AM the wind was howling and sounded like the proverbial railroad train. It was a constant roar, and there was no way to sleep. The house was vibrating, and I was afraid if it got much worse, things were going to start flying off the house. The girls were awake too, so we brought them downstairs, so that we would all be on the first floor for safety reasons. Somewhere around three AM it went dead quiet. We figured that we must be in the eye of the storm, so we ventured outside onto the front porch with flashlights. The first thing that I noticed was how hot and muggy it was, and it was very still. We couldn't tell much in the dark, but I noticed that the north side of the house was completely covered with pine straw and leaves, almost like paper- mache'. One of the girls pointed to the two ceiling fans on the porch, and we noticed that all of the paddles were gone. I guess that the wind had them spinning so fast that the centrifugal force pulled them off. The next morning, we found them spread from the house all the way out to the barn, 150 yards away. Still no sign of Jenny, and I started to wonder if we would ever see her again. We went back inside and battened down for the second half of the storm and tried to get some sleep. The back side was not a severe as the front side, thank goodness.

When I looked out the kitchen window the next morning, I was not prepared for what I saw. It looked like a war zone. There were trees and parts of trees down everywhere and I could tell that the metal roof had blown off the large hay barn where we had just stored our hay for the winter. My first reaction was, "My God, the whole forest has blown down!!" I was truly shocked by what I saw, since I had not heard a single tree come down during the night. I went to the front porch to check on the horses, and thankfully they were all clustered together in the middle of the pasture. Instinctively they knew to get out of the woods, which was smart because the woods appeared to be pretty much blown flat. Johnny's house across the pond appeared to be okay, and I could see that most of the cows were clustered in the field behind his house. Just then, I noticed old Jenny trotting across the pasture as though nothing had happened. Glory be! We thought she was a goner for sure!

Johnny Johnson surveying some of the damage the morning after

As the morning wore on, we realized that we had a full-blown emergency on our hands! Johnny and I had walked around and surveyed the damage around the fields where the cows and horses were. Every stretch of fence line was breeched somewhere with trees on them. The first order of business was going to be securing the animals before they started to wander, and to make sure that they had full access to water, which meant the ponds since we had no power to run the wells . At that that time, we had about 60 head of cows and two bulls and five or six horses, so we mostly spent that first day securing them. We had no electricity, which meant no water, and from the looks of things, it could be days or weeks before it was restored. It turned out to be right at two weeks. There was no phone service, and it was pre cell phones, so we could not communicate with anyone that was not here. The phone service came back on in a couple of days, which was a big help.

I knew that we had a catastrophe in the forest but really had not had a chance to assess, because we were so busy trying to secure the livestock. In the early afternoon of that first day, Angus pulled up to where Johnny and I were working on the fence. The worst of the storm had been east of Columbia, and had apparently tracked up the Wateree, instead of the Congaree as had been predicted. Angus was headed east checking on clients, and we were the first of his clients that apparently had major damage. Boy was I glad to see him!

"Looks like you got a real problem Cate," he said. "I'll make some calls tonight, and try to get a logger in here soon," he added, then headed back out to move further east to check on other clients. We went back to work securing fencing. The next job for that first day was hauling water in buckets for washing and flushing and making sure that we had lanterns for that first night.

Once we felt that the animals were in at least in a temporarily secure and safe spot, we started wandering around on foot looking at the damage, trying to get a better handle on just what we were dealing with. I was very tired by then and it was very depressing. Johnny and I were down around the Duck Pond, looking at the fence there, when our friend Drew Robb showed up riding a bicycle that he had ridden down from where he lived at Cooks Mountain. Drew worked for the SC Department of Natural Resources (DNR) and lived on and was caretaker for Yancey and Robin McLeod at Cooks Mountain at the time. He said that there were so many trees across the 3.5 mile stretch of road between here and there that he could have walked as easily as riding the bike because he had to lift the bike over so many of them. We commiserated for a little while and then Drew headed home, but not before brightening our spirits a bit. He has a very dry wit and left us with some refreshing fox hole humor before departing. To this day, Drew and I still laugh about that impromptu conference the afternoon after Hugo. I felt better as I headed back up the hill to the barn to start preparing for the night. We went to bed early because there was nothing to do, and we knew that the next day was going to be another long one.

Saturday was spent cutting up and using the tractor to drag off the trees and larger limbs from our yard and trying to get around the rest of the Farm to assess the extent of the damage. After two days, the only place we could drive to was out to the paved road. All other farm roads were blocked with trees and debris. That meant that this survey had to be performed on foot, or to get to the more remote spots, I saddled my horse, Sir, and rode him. This was very effective and served me well until we could get some of the other roads open, which looked like it was going to be a while.

Hay barn and paddocks – notice the missing roof of the barn

Oddly, luckily, none of the houses on the Farm were badly damaged, and other than the aforementioned barn roof, the other farm buildings were spared. Oh, there was some blown up tin, or shingles missing, but the real damage was in the forest, and of course, the fences.

115

Some of the damage near the back of the farm house

More of the damage

Sometime before Sunday, the phone service was restored, and we began contact with the outside world. The most important call I got was from Angus, who said that he had a logging crew lined up, and wanted me to meet with him, Gordon, and the logger Monday morning when he was moving his crew in. We decided to start at the entrance to the Farm House off of Cate Road, and cut out from there. That was the logical starting point, because you could not drive a vehicle to the house anyway because of the large number of trees across the road.

Angus, Gordon, and I met with Allen Brock from Holmes Timber and his logger at the front mailbox Monday morning as planned. We agreed on a price, and they went to work. It was slow going. They were here for three months. We all were having to learn and adapt as we went. None of us had ever dealt with something of this scale. Most of our downed trees were just blown over and not broken off, so for the most part, the wood itself was not damaged. But because of the angle, the cutting machine could not get the saw blade on the tree to cut it. The meant that the cutting machine was going to be useless in this operation, so the crew had to first go out and buy some chainsaws to cut the trees from the stump. Then the skidder could attach to the tree and drag it to the deck. Fortunately, almost all of our downed trees were lying in the same direction, that being from the northeast to the southwest. It was at this point that I said, "I'll never need a compass on this place again. All I have to do is find a root ball and know that the front side is facing southwest, and the back side is facing northeast."

It was amazing how much better I started to feel about things, once the salvage operation began. For one thing, I started noticing the standing trees instead just the ones that were blown down, and just like that, my cup went from half empty to half full! When our salvage was completed, I realized how lucky we were compared to other landowners that had similar, or even more damage. We figured that we had about 40% of our standing timber blown down. It was very random of course, and usually it was the best timber that blew down first. Oddly, some coves were missed almost entirely, and some areas were blown flat. One 30-acre stand did not have a tree standing except for a few broken off snags.

All in all, we had a very good salvage compared to others. For starters, we got a favorable price given the circumstances, about 70% of the pre-Hugo price. We got a decent price because we got started quickly, due to Angus and Gordon's fast action getting a logger lined up. As days and weeks went by, the price dropped steadily all the way to zero as desperate landowners were willing to give the wood away, just to get it removed. All of this was further complicated, in that about two weeks after the hurricane, we had a huge rainstorm in the upper coastal plain. As I recall, we had like 18 inches of rain in three days, and this caused some really serious flooding in many areas that completely halted the salvage for many landowners. At the Farm, there was always some loggable ground that our crew could move to. It did slow the process down however. As it turned out, we were able to salvage most of our better timber. I figured that we salvaged 90% of the sawtimber, 50% of the pulpwood, and none of the hardwood. The loggers would at least pull it out of the way if it was blocking something. We worked on it for firewood for the next five years, I guess. As far as our salvage went, we fared better than almost anyone I have talked with about it. Again, I credit Angus and Gordon for their fast action.

The balance of the cleanup was a very painful experience. Fortunately, I was only 45 years old and had plenty of energy. Most of Johnny's time, and all of my free time for the next ten months was spent cutting up and hauling off debris or fixing permanent fencing. I remember one Saturday afternoon the following July, and several chainsaws later, telling Johnny after we had cut a tree out of a fence below the Duck Pond and repaired the fence, "That's it! We have cut our last Hugo tree. Mother Nature will have to do the rest!!"

Hurricane Hugo completely changed the way we viewed and managed our forest. It caused us to intensify our management efforts. Areas that we previously did not manage at all, suddenly were very much part of our management plan. And we had learned not to get too attached to any particular patch of woods, because something can occur to cause it to go away in one night's time! I must say that the intensified efforts paid serious dividends, and within five years' time, I could say with certainty, that our forest had never looked better!

The Great Flood of 2015

In October of 2015, the remnants of Hurricane Joaquin caused an unusual low-pressure system to settle over central South Carolina and just sit there for several days. The weather service had it right for once and predicted rainfall of 12 to 15 inches of rainfall over that period. Well, the Eastover neighborhood ended up being "ground zero" for the event which dumped 21 inches of rain on the Farm that weekend.

That was on top of the seven inches of rain that occurred the weekend before when a freak thunderstorm sat on our end of Richland County all night. The earlier storm had already created significant damage to our roads. Bottom line was we had 28 inches of rain in eight days. These numbers were unheard of in my lifetime. The event created massive flooding in neighborhoods all over central South Carolina.

Flood damage taking place
All flood photos are furnished by William Cate

Many families lost their homes in the flooding in what was frequently described as the "1,000-year flood". While our buildings were secure, other than a few roof leaks that we didn't know we had, we had significant damage to four ponds as well as most of our roads and infrastructure. One pond dam breeched completely and had to be rebuilt, and the other three were still holding water but seriously damaged and required extensive repairs. Several roads were completely blown out, including the road to our house. Like with Hugo, we were left to figure out what to do on our own.

We knew that we were going to have some very costly repairs to our dams and infrastructure at the Farm. Fortunately, I already had Hawthorne Construction lined up to replace some pipe for us, so I called James Hawthorne and told him that I was going to need a lot more work than just replacing some pipe. I asked that James come over and look at it with me, and come up with a ballpark figure of what it was going to cost. After studying it for a while, he figured that we had somewhere in the neighborhood of $100,000 worth of work to get everything fixed. The first thing that needed to happen was James his son, Sam and a crew, come and do a temporary fix on the main road to our house, before starting to fix the ponds. Our road was completely undrivable as it was. We left Betsy's car out on the pavement, one-half mile away, and she could access it using our UTV, going out an alternate route through a lot of mud. I could drive my big truck out the back way to US601, but the road deteriorated further with each trip, as it was a lot of slipping and sliding.

Breached dam

Flood damage on road to our house

The next thing we needed to do was figure out how we were going to pay for all of this. In keeping with our philosophy of having the Farm pay its own way, we knew,

120

of course, that the best way to raise some money, was to cut enough timber to cover what we needed. I called Gordon the next day, and he met me that week at the Farm to identify some stands that made sense to liquidate and attempt to get the best bang for the buck while doing so. We fairly quickly agreed on three separate stands totaling about 95 acres that we selected for one or more of the following reasons. They needed to be accessible to roads and be reasonably dry sites (Remember that we had just had 28 inches of rain). There was something that we did not like about the stand that could be fixed when we reforested, such as seeding in around the edges, causing it to be overstocked. Or in one case, the stand was about 40 years old and had essentially stopped growing. Gordon called Bob Crittenden with Hentz Forest Products and asked if Clyde Brown, the owner of Mount Bethel Logging was available. Clyde had recently done some harvesting for us, and we found him to be most accommodating and conscientious. He was available and moved in several days later, and like with Hugo, as soon as the logging and the repair work began, there was great relief that we were going to get everything fixed, and that we were going to be able to pay for it. Clyde's crew was here for about two months, and Sam and James Hawthorne were on the Farm for about three, finishing up just after Christmas.

We were back good as new except for the reforestation of the 95 acres that had been clear cut. That would take place over the next years' time. Those stands are now several years old, and they are already obviously better that the ones that they are replacing.

Pine Beetles

This last catastrophic event I started not to even mention in that it is hardly known of at all except to those landowners that it happened to. In 2019, it had rained all winter and spring, creating very wet conditions. Then in mid-July, the rain basically stopped at the Farm for the next three months and the rest of the summer became very hot with daily temperatures running from 90 to 100 degrees all the way into mid-October.

Imagine watering your centipede grass every day, which you are not supposed to do, because you would be over-watering it. Then stop watering for two months and see what happens to it. Well, that is what was going on in our woods late in the summer of 2019. Individual trees became highly stressed. Stressed trees become susceptible to pine beetle infestation. Ips beetles will typically attack a stressed or damaged pine tree like after a lightning strike or similar event. When they have killed that tree, they will usually move to several neighboring trees, and then die out. So, usually, only four or five trees die out in a group.

We first noticed some random dead mature pines by the end of July. Then we noticed a 25-year-old pine plantation that had a lot of dead or dying trees in it. I would notice that stand every time I left the farm, and by now was paying close attention. I soon realized there were new dying trees showing up in the stand every day and was noticing more random groups of dying trees scattered around the Farm, and was reaching the conclusion that we had a real problem developing, and it seemed to be happening in mature sawtimber stands.

I put in a call to Gordon Baker, and he was here the next day. As we rode around the Farm, we realized quickly it was much worse that originally thought. We found three stands of mature plantation pines that were mostly dead or dying. Two of the stands were roughly 25 years old, and the third was 40 years old. They were mostly sawtimber if the wood wasn't too far gone. We found random bug spots all around the property and it appeared to be getting worse by the day. There was quite a bit of damage around our house. It was obvious that we were going to need a fairly large timber salvage operation, and soon! We faced several major issues. First, it was so hot that the wood was deteriorating by the day. We wanted to harvest as much of the sawtimber as possible because it is the highest value product. If the tree was actually dead, it would be downgraded to pulpwood, so we wanted to get started as soon as possible. The other two issues were that the sawtimber pricing was terrible, and the mills had everyone on tight quotas, so it was really hard to get wood cut at that time. We had already been waiting on another logging operation for over a year. It created a very worrisome dilemma. If we were not able to get the wood harvested, it would truly be a mess. Gordon worked some magic, called in a couple of favors, and the next day Rick Kernan with Almond Forest Products was on the site with a real good logging crew, led by Steven Sims. The price was not good, but we knew it wouldn't be. They had plenty of quota and could start right away. We made a deal, and they went right to work and I immediately started to feel better, just like after Hugo and the Great Flood. Having those bugs in my trees, and not being able to do anything about it was driving me nuts. I would wake up in the night worrying about it. It was like having pigs in my cornfield or army worms in my hayfield.

Having them begin working was a great relief, and they did a good job of moving around the Farm and getting to most of the areas that were worst hit with the beetles. Sometimes we would give them some extra good wood along with the damaged in order to make it worth their while to move to that site. We even removed about twenty trees from our yard, some right next to our house!

Although these three catastrophic events were completely different in nature and scope, they share a common denominator. They each caused us to cut a lot more wood at the time than we normally would have and put our future sustainability plan at risk. In other words, it put us out of sync for a few years, and will require some extra management discipline to get over the immediate horizon.

Duck Supper

One of the more unusual traditions that takes place at the Farm each year is the annual Duck Supper that Betsy and I put on each year. The event takes place at the Farm House each December on the Saturday before Christmas unless that is Christmas Eve, and then we back it up a week. The same friends have been invited each year and have been for many years.

The Duck Supper got it's start without a lot of forethought (none actually), and at the time we certainly didn't know that we were starting a tradition that would go on for nearly 60 years. Let's start with the first one. While home from college for Christmas break in December 1962, my old friends, Angus Lafaye and Barron Grier, and I had had a very successful duck hunt while camping on the upper reaches of Cane Branch on Lake Marion in the Santee Swamp. While sitting around the camp fire, we were discussing what to do with all of those ducks. I said, "My mother has a great duck recipe! Let's call Ellison and Gunter, round up the girls and go to the Farm and cook them!"

The first Duck Supper took place on Christmas Eve of 1962. The participants were myself and Vinnie Seibels, Angus Lafaye and Carolyn Jackson, Barron Grier and Susan Rigby, Jimmy Gunter and Norrie Nicholson, and Ellison Smith and Diane Cartledge. I think that I have all of the girls matched up appropriately. It was a blast! The ducks turned out great, and everybody had so much fun, that without realizing that we were creating a tradition, we agreed that we would do the same thing, same time next year.

The second Duck Supper was even more fun! That was

Founding fathers, Billy and Angus – 1962 or 1963

when the gag gift tradition began. We drew names and gave whoever you drew a funny present. The crowd was the same, although a couple of the dates didn't make the cut. I am sure that Vinnie, Diane, and Susan were there, however I am not sure who the other two girls were. Unfortunately, very few photos remain of the very early ones. Of course, we didn't know at the time that we were creating something special. Over the next several years, the Duck Supper began to evolve. The biggest part of that evolution happened in 1964 when I came home from Vermont with Betsy Walker, and she assumed the role of "hostess" of the Duck Supper.

It changed again in 1967. Betsy and I were home on leave from the army after being gone for a year. We wanted to see some friends, so we expanded the group to include Barry Meyer, John Lumpkin, Tom Milliken, Cal and Francis McMeekin, and Billy and Joy Bruner. The unattached guys brought dates, some of which later became wives and/or former wives.

After most of us started having children the event was moved from Christmas Eve to the Saturday before Christmas. The group continued to expand over the next several years, and by the middle of the 1970s, the Duck Supper had 13 couples. They were Jimmy and Lucy Gunter, Ellison and Diane Smith,

Duck Supper 1967

Duck Supper 1968

Duck Supper 1983

Barron and Judy Grier, Angus and Cary Lafaye, Billy and Joy Bruner, Cal and Francis McMeekin, John and Emily Lumpkin. Tom and Anne Milliken, Barry and Diane Meyer, Woody and Julia Moore, Yancey and Robin McLeod, Johnny and Katherine Mahon, and of course, Betsy and myself.

Well, the years flew by, and before we knew it, the Duck Supper had evolved into something truly special, with unique

Duck Supper 1997

Duck Supper 2016

traditions. For starters, the only rule is…" that you can't change any rules!" It takes place in the same timeless house. We have the same menu each year, we give some really stupid presents, and each year, we gather in front of the fireplace, and take a group photo. The group photo has become one of the real treasures where you can see the same group of friends age in the same setting and enjoy the changes to clothing and hair styles.

At the fortieth Duck Supper Betsy and I gave everyone a calendar which commemorated some of the classic photos scattered across the years. At the fiftieth one, everyone received a fleece vest signifying the event.

50th Anniversary Vest

We are now much closer to the 60th Duck Supper than the 50th. The last 15 years or so have taken a toll on our group of lifelong friends. Sadly, four of these dear friends have passed away. Billy Bruner in 2006, Barry Meyer in 2008, Jimmy Gunter in 2009, and Robin McLeod in 2017. Each one has left a big hole in our group. Betsy and I have discussed this for years, but there is simply no way to perpetuate this special occasion forever. There is no way to pass it on to the next generation. It is for us anyway, not them. Picking the appropriate time to stop any meaningful activity is always difficult. Believing strongly that it is always better go out on top if possible, the 60th Duck Supper will be the last.

Wildlife

Remember that we have three main priorities that we have used for as long as I can remember in the management of our Farm. They are, in order, timber production, wildlife management, and aesthetics. We never make a management decision without considering all three. That said, wildlife, and the management of, and for the benefit of, has been a common theme throughout our lives on the Farm.

What has changed over the years, is the type of wildlife that we are managing, both game, and nongame species. When I was a boy, we had a lot of Bobwhite Quail (birds), doves (if you managed for them), a few deer, and no turkeys. Once some habitat was provided, we always had a few ducks. From a nongame perspective, there were no beavers, no coyotes, no armadillos, a few alligators, very few eagles. And believe it or not, there weren't even many squirrels. My theory on the squirrels is that the neighborhood hunted them hard for food, along with some other critters.

Today we certainly have no shortage of squirrels. In addition, the Farm supports a large population of fox squirrels, which I confess is probably my favorite mammal, next to dogs, of course! They are about twice the size of their grey cousins and sport a long flowing tail. They come in a variety of colors, from jet black to silver to red, often with some white trim, or in a combination of the above.

What has really changed over the last 60 years or so, is the disappearance of the quail (birds). In reality, they were probably already beginning to disappear when I was hunting them as a boy and remembered great quantities of coveys on our land. Their decline was happening so gradually, that we just did not

Fox Squirrel by Jane Willcox Salley

realize it at the time it was happening. What has happened
to them? Well, there are many, many opinions. Some based
on well documented scientific research, some based on pure
speculation, many times based on little more than personal
bias. We hear things like there are too many hawks and owls,
too many coyotes, too many feral cats or todays clean farming
techniques. We hear strong opinions that it is the fire ants,
or the cattle egrets. While it is true that these two critters
(fire ants and cattle egrets) showed up in great numbers in
South Carolina in the 1970s, about the time that my family
was beginning to notice that the birds definitely were on the
decline.

I think that the truth is a lot more complicated than
any one answer. All these theories may have some merit and
may have contributed to varying degrees to the decline. My
own theory is that the decline of the birds is the result of
a combination of many factors working against them, and
eventually overwhelming the population, and I feel strongly
that the biggest single issue is the massive landscape changes
in both forestry and agriculture over the last 100 years. The
heyday for the bobwhite was when the one-horse farm (40
acres and a mule) was most prevalent. That period is primarily
from the end of the American Civil War until just after World

War II. The countryside was just a patchwork of these small subsistence type farms. These were rough farms, worked mostly with mules, and very different from the large-scale agricultural operations that we see today. These small farms created lots of edge effect and lots of weeds, briars, and dense ground cover. Birds have a lot of predators. They are ground nesters, therefore are vulnerable to many types of predation. There are lots of critters that would love to eat a baby quail or a quail egg. To successfully nest, birds need very dense ground cover and lots of it. These small farms created the perfect environment for the birds.

What caused all of this to change? We've already discussed how the sharecropper, tenant farmer system in the South began to breakdown in the 1920s and 30s and was almost completely gone by the mid-1950s. The demise of this system of agriculture almost immediately started to stress the habitat for the bobwhite quail, although it took many more years for the impact to be fully realized. The reason for this is that many (most really) of these abandoned farms remained in place for many years after the inhabitants left. The landscape gradually began to change, but in the meantime, it provided the perfect place for "Mr. Bob" to live and prosper. For as long as we hunted birds on our Farm, we were most likely to find a covey around one of these old homesteads. In fact, we actually

Me (L) and Charlie (My father) bird hunting in late 1970's
Photo by William (Bill) C. Boyd

named those coveys for the family that had once lived on those abandoned farms. I think we would find this pattern existed across the entire Southeast.

The demise of the preferred habitat for the Bobwhite Quail brought about improved habitat for other species, namely White-tail Deer and Eastern Wild Turkey. Over the decades that the bobwhite was gradually disappearing across South Carolina, the Whitetail Deer and the Eastern Wild Turkey were surging. This was happening for the same reasons that the birds were declining. The deer and the turkey have much larger home ranges than do quail. The birds were healthy and happy sharing the landscape with the subsistence farmers on our Farm, as well as farms across South Carolina and the Southeast. That landscape was not compatible with the deer and turkeys that much prefer large expanse of woodlands and fields, especially as these species were trying to re-establish themselves.

By the end of the 1940s there were no turkeys and only a few deer in the area around our Farm in central South Carolina. But also, the small subsistence farms were by then mostly abandoned, and were gradually becoming huge areas of woodlands, with very large acreages owned by the US Forest Service or the paper companies that had moved into South Carolina in the 1930s and 40s. These companies bought up much of the land that had once been small farms to produce a company-owned wood supply to be used to feed the paper mills that were being built across the Southeast. In the early 1950's The South Carolina Department of Natural Resources (SCDNR) successfully relocated deer and turkeys, principally from the Francis Marion National Forest, to the sprawling Sumter National Forest in the Upstate. These new populations quickly reestablished themselves and began to spread.

On our Farm, which is situated in the Wateree portion of the COWASEE Basin in the upper coastal plain, the same pattern existed as in the piedmont except that the deer never completely disappeared. The few deer that remained lived mostly in or near the river swamp. The turkeys had been gone since the 1930's. The small farms that had made up our land had been consolidated into a much larger land holding and was becoming mostly woodlands and much more conducive to supporting the deer herd that was expanding out of the river swamps. By the 1950s we were beginning to regularly see deer on our land. Over the next 45 years this herd would expand exponentially until the mid to late 1990s when it began to level off.

Charlie (my father) had always said that some of his fondest memories were of turkey hunting at Goodwill as a boy and as a young man. He dreamed that someday, there would be a huntable population again. Sometime in the early 1970s, Charlie read a Sunday newspaper article that DNR was planning to initiate a program to trap turkeys on state and federal land that had established, healthy populations and to relocate them on private land for the first time in areas that had no viable turkey populations. Charlie seized upon that article and Monday morning brought it to the office and showed it to me. Soon after our conversation he was calling DNR to learn some details about the program. He was put in touch with Vernon Bevill, a biologist, who was the Turkey Project Coordinator for DNR. Vernon told Charlie that a requirement for participation in the turkey relocation program was 15,000 acres contiguous acres, but that he would be happy to meet with us to discuss the program and to look around the surrounding neighborhood.

At that time, a group of family and friends had a long-term hunting lease on Goodwill next to our farm, so we controlled about 4500 acres of what we thought was suitable habitat to support a wild turkey flock. We were on good terms with two large hunting clubs adjoining our acreage, Cooks Mountain Hunting Club to the north that controlled about 8,000 acres and Eastover Hunting Club to the east across the Wateree River. I reached out to John Wolfe, the president of Cooks Mountain Club, and to Bill Czarnitsky, who was about Charlie's age and had grown up hunting turkeys as a young man. Bill was a longtime member of the Eastover Hunting Club which controlled another 5,000 acres across the Wateree River. Both clubs were old timey dog driving clubs, but both men were very interested in throwing in with us if we could work some sort of deal out with DNR.

Vernon, Charlie, and I met for lunch at the old Coronet Motel near the Farm in 1971 or 1972 and spent the afternoon riding around the Farm and Goodwill as he did a preliminary site assessment. He really perked up when he saw the property and learned of the possibility of adding the additional acreage. He explained the process to us and said that it may take several years for the plan to come together. The plan was to look at as many potential suitable sites as possible and to select several for the first wave of relocations. Another site group would be selected for the following year and each year following that until they felt that there were enough flocks out there that they could sustain themselves.

Vernon and I became fast friends, and he would come over a couple of times a year as he worked on his assessments. He would usually come in the fall and we would go deer hunting. He took me turkey hunting in Edgefield County. Over the next several years, we organized our consortium of adjoining landowners and the hunting clubs that controlled the leases on the land. This in itself was no small feat!

The way it was to work, DNR lawyers were responsible for preparing an agreement that was to be signed by each of the adjoining landowners in the consortium as well as the person authorized for each of the hunting clubs. I was designated as the point person to coordinate our group. DNR was to trap turkeys from Francis Marion National Forest or the Savannah River Plant and relocate them to the selected sites. The landowners and clubs agreed that there would be no hunting of turkeys for five years or until DNR said that there could be a season. They further agreed that in the event of a successful stocking resulting in an increasing population, DNR had the right for a number of years to come back and to trap some of the turkeys and relocate them to another site to further enhance the restoration process.

We learned sometime in early 1976 that we were selected to be in the first wave of five sites to receive birds, likely within the next year. We learned in the fall of that year, that we were to be Site Number One! By then we were really beginning to get excited.

Between Christmas and New Year in 1976, seven turkeys were trapped from Francis Marion and delivered to Goodwill and released in a field just behind our clubhouse. Representatives of all of the cooperators in our group were there to watch. During the first week of 1977, eight more were trapped and released at the same site. In our release there were 15 birds total, eight hens and seven gobblers.

One interesting side note of this story is that when the turkeys were being released, radio tracking collars were installed on about half of them. I rode with Vernon as we tracked them

Turkey release at Goodwill – 1976

to their roost site. Oddly, we tracked I think three to Basins Landing, the spot overlooking the river where Charlie had killed his first turkey in 1916 at age 15. For the next several years, Basins Landing was the best area to spot a turkey and it was a favorite roost site. To this day, it remains a prime spot to sight a gobbler.

Needless to say, the turkey stocking program has been wildly successful, and is one of the outstanding environmental success stories in this state. Charlie would be astounded to know that there are more wild turkeys in South Carolina today than Bobwhite Quail.

Forty plus years after the wild turkey project, Buckeye Farms participated in another endangered bird relocation project. This time we were going from moving very large birds to moving very small ones. The Red-cockaded Woodpecker (RCW) has been on the endangered species list for many years. Their decline stemmed from habitat loss as is usually the case. RCW's require very specialized habitat. Namely, they need mature southern yellow pine for their nest and roost trees. When I say mature, I mean at least 60 to 80 years of age. The den trees must be in an area that have little or no mid-story. Each cluster (three or four cavities) of den trees needs to be supported by approximately 75 acres of suitable foraging habitat which consist of mature and semi-mature pine woodlands with a mostly open mid-story. By mid-story I mean the area between 20 and 45 feet in height as this is the primary feeding area of the RCW's. They fly through these open woodlands and collect insects from the pine bark at these height levels.

Red-cockaded Woodpecker by Jim Kelly

My lifelong friend, Angus Lafaye has been involved with the Longleaf Alliance for many years, serving first as a board member and then as chairman. The primary mission of the Longleaf Alliance is the restoration of the longleaf pine to its natural range across the southeast. Along with this goal is restoration of animal species that are dependent on highly specialized longleaf habitat. The Red-cockaded Woodpecker (RCW) is one of these species. The Longleaf Alliance, along with the US Fish and Wildlife Service, and the SC Department of Natural Resources secured a sizable grant to fund the relocation of surplus RCWs from government lands that had suitable populations and move them to private landowners that were willing to accept and take care of the birds. These landowner's property needed to have the right amount of suitable habitat to support the RCW's but be land that did not presently have any.

Angus, being very familiar with every aspect of our land, recommended us as a candidate. He asked if we would like to participate, and we enthusiastically accepted. Like the turkey project, forty years before, the process took several years to come together. Once again, there was a fairly lengthy assessment period to look at the available sites across the state in the traditional longleaf range. In the end, our farm was selected for the first group of 5 or 6 properties to receive RCW's. Our property and one other from the COWASEE Basin were chosen. The selection committee included Lisa Lord with LLA, Caroline Causey with DNR, Ralph Costa, Angus, and several others. Ralph is retired from the Fish and Wildlife Service, as well as from Clemson University and wrote what is probably the most complete work on RCW recovery, *Red Cockaded Woodpecker Road to Recovery*. They especially liked our property because of the good longleaf habitat and the fact that we were just 5 miles southeast of Fort Jackson where there was already a viable population of RCW's. The thinking there was that there might be an opportunity for some cross-pollination between groups.

The plan was to trap three pairs of juvenile RCW's and deliver them to each of the three clusters of den sites sometime in early November 2018. Before that could be done, cavities had to be inserted into the den trees in each cluster, with each cluster to contain four cavities.

Cavity insert

Larry Wood, a contractor for the Fish and Wildlife Service was hired to install the cavity boxes, which was a very interesting process to watch, each box being installed in the selected den trees at about 25 feet in height. That was done in early November.

We were informed that our birds would be coming the week before Thanksgiving on Tuesday night. The way it was supposed to work, a group of volunteers would catch the three pairs at Francis Marion National Forest just after they flew up to roost, prepare them for travel, and to head to the Farm with their cargo, expecting to arrive around eleven. Each pair would be going to a different cluster, and since most of the volunteer group had never been on our

Cavities being installed

land before, it was necessary to provide a guide for each group to lead them in the dark to the selected den trees so the RCW's could be inserted into their particular cavity. My nephew, Charlie, son Walker and myself provided the guide service. Once inserted, a screen was tacked over the entrance hole with an attached rope dangling down to the ground. This was done to keep the birds safe and secure overnight in their new surroundings, while they acclimated and oriented themselves. At daybreak the next morning the groups went back to their assigned cluster and pulled the screens off with the attached rope, and the 6 birds were free to come and go as the pleased.

So far, there have been mixed results. One cluster has successfully raised fledglings two years running, and we put 4 more birds out last fall in the other two clusters. There is evidence of some activity in both of them. One of the RCW's from the first stocking has shown up at Fort Jackson, 5 miles away. Hopefully, they will ultimately continue to do well and thrive. While the RCW restoration is very different from the turkey restoration, as was the motivation for doing so, the sense of accomplishment is much the same. It is very satisfying to have such a fragile endangered species surviving in the habitat on our Farm.

There are some other non-game critters that have shown up over the last 50 years or so that I am not so thrilled about. I have already mentioned the infamous fire ants and cattle egrets, but we now have lots of alligators (and very large ones), wild pigs, coyotes, beavers, armadillos, and a variety of invasive plant species, all combining to pose threats to the species we are trying to protect, and adding greatly to the management challenges to our operation. For example, a drove of wild hogs can root up a field with holes that you could hide a Volkswagen in. They make it impossible to plant corn unless the field is fenced to keep them out. Needless to

Birds being inserted

say, coyotes will kill and eat anything they can catch. If all of these dynamic changes can happen in our wildlife populations over the last 60 years or so, who knows, maybe Mr. Bob will come back!

Protection Efforts

There are many terrible problems in our country and in the world today. Of course, I worry about them, as I am sure everyone does, no matter what their viewpoint might be. But I have come to realize that it doesn't matter how much these issues concern me, I can't fix these problems, no matter how hard I try, or how much I worry. I think most people are frustrated by these "World View" issues that they can't do anything about. Fifteen years ago, when I went to work for the Congaree Land Trust as Executive Director and became involved with the COWASEE Basin Task Force, I realized that I could use that platform to meaningfully affect some conservation activities that would directly benefit my own back yard.

The COWASEE Basin Task Force was established in 2005 with a goal to establish the Basin (315,000 acres along the Congaree, Wateree, and Santee Rivers) as a major focus area in parts of five counties in the upper coastal plain in the central part of South Carolina. The idea was to pattern the project after the highly successful ACE Basin in the low country. I was highly energized by this prospect not only as a a landowner in the Basin, but it represented the heart of my lifelong stomping grounds. I also saw it as an opportunity to become a project that the Congaree Land Trust could rally around and focus on as a primary part of their mission. Up until this time, CLT had been using a shotgun approach in its nine county area with no real focus to the way they targeted easements. By this time, our Farm was under a conservation easement and had been for several years.

As already mentioned in the chapter on The COWASEE

Basin, roughly 50% of the 315,000 acres has been protected, either publicly or privately. I am particularly proud of the work that has been done along the Wateree Corridor in COWASEE along both sides of the Wateree River, mainly in Richland and Sumter Counties, but also in the lower portions of Kershaw County.

I say that I am proud of the work done in this area, meaning that I am very pleased with the outcomes, as it matches up with my objectives when I first went into the conservation business. But let me be clear, we had a lot of help making these projects come together. Different strategies are required for each one of these conservation projects, as the needs and desires of the individual landowners varied greatly. I have always felt that the Congaree Land Trust served as the linchpin to create the success we have had throughout COWASEE, particularly along the Wateree. Executive Director, Stuart White, and Land Protection Director, Mary Crockett have been extremely supportive and influential. Major funding for grants that help many of these deals happen has come from the Department of Defense, Jason Johnson with the Conservation Fund, The South Carolina Conservation Bank, and from the Dorothy and Edward Kendall Foundation. In addition, many individuals worked tirelessly to tie some of these projects together, creating vital connectivity that greatly enhances the conservation value of individual conservation easements. James Hugh Ryan, retired South Carolina State Forester and member of the COWASEE Basin Task Force, lives on his family's historic farm near Wedgefield in Sumter County. He did a magnificent job pulling nine of his immediate neighbors together doing nine separate conservation easements in what is known as the Mine Hill Project. Angus Lafaye with Milliken Forestry and Roy Belser with American Forest Management, both members of the COWASEE Basin Task Force, recognized an opportunity for some of their larger clients to conserve their land and benefit not only themselves but also the Department of Defense, the state of South Carolina, and the general public.

You might ask yourself why the Department of Defense is interested in conserving land along this part of the Wateree. Well, the area that we are describing here is uniquely sandwiched between four important military bases. The bases are Fort Jackson and McEntire National Guard

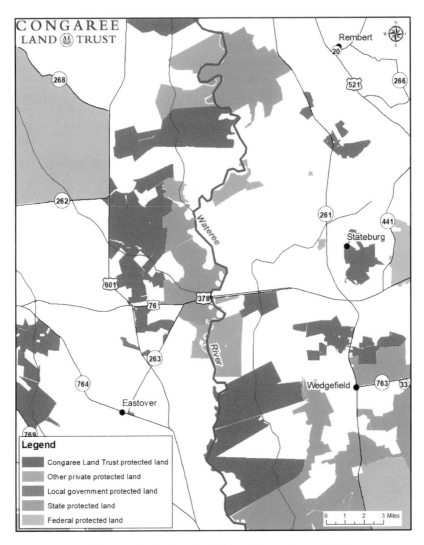

Protected lands along the Wateree River, January 2021

Map prepared by Mark Lowery

Base in Richland County, and Shaw Air Force Base and Poinsett Bombing Range in Sumter County. About the time that COWASEE was getting cranked up, the Department of Defense was beginning to recognize the value of protecting land that was at risk of being developed around important bases. They did not want to wake up 10 or 20 years down the road and realize that they could no longer perform their mission because of encroaching development. A consortium was formed between local officials from the City of Columbia and Richland County, and from the City of Sumter and Sumter County as well civilian and military representatives from each of the bases. These four bases are very important economic engines in both of these communities, so the overall health of the bases is very important to them. Representatives from the Army, the Air Force, and the National Guard, as well as the Conservation Fund and the Congaree Land Trust all are part of the consortium. It is called MAJIC, which is your prototypical military acronym for Midlands Area Joint Installation Consortium. MAJIC has been a major component in the conservation successes that we have had in the area described.

Closer to home, I am proud to say there is now more than 12,000 contiguous acres of protected land in the area surrounding our Farm. This is huge for the neighborhood, as it insures for the future the same landscape flavor that I have known and enjoyed all my life. It ensures that our children and grandchildren, and their children also, will have the same opportunities to enjoy this same flavor. In my view, the conservation success in our local neighborhood is more than I could have hoped for when I first got involved. Granted, there is much work yet to be done, and plenty more opportunities are out there! To those that say that the process is too slow, and that conservation success should happen at a faster pace, I say that there is no finish line in this business. We protect these properties one at a time, and we should celebrate each one as a victory!

The Challenge

Having spent a lifetime in a family business and managing a family farm, I feel well qualified to address the challenges faced by both types of endeavors. These challenges take many forms. Just operating a farm or a business successfully in the first place is challenging enough, but transferring that success from generation to generation is where the really tough challenge is. As I said, I have been looking at these issues for most of my life, and I am well aware of what the statistics say. Statistically, very few family owned businesses or farms make it to the third generation, much less through it. I can say without hesitation that a farm or family business will not make it through the third generation without careful planning.

There are many reasons why this is so difficult. Let's start with the founder of a farm or business. Such endeavors usually begin with someone with an entrepreneurial spirit that truly loves what they do. They are willing to work hard enough to overcome just about any adversity. If they make it for the first couple of years, they have a pretty good chance at success. When it comes to a generational shift in the ownership and operation of the enterprise, the next crowd may or may not have someone with the aptitude and leadership to successfully replace the founder. By the third generation, the numbers of people involved severely complicate the ownership and decision-making process, and that usually requires some sort of structural change.

Since this book is about farms, and in particular our Farm, that is what this chapter will focus on instead of other types of family businesses. In my work with the Congaree Land Trust, I frequently met with families that were in the second, third or even fourth generation of ownership, that had very weak systems of management and no clear path as to what were the best ways to transfer ownership when the time came. With all the family dynamics that can come into play with multiple owners of an extremely valuable asset, it is very important to have a good plan. As previously mentioned, I have frequently encountered landowners that inherited a really good piece of land with their siblings, and yet many years later, still had no idea what they were trying to accomplish or any kind of system of priorities. This, even in light of the fact that the land might represent the family's most valuable asset. In my view, the worst thing that can happen to a good piece of land is for the family after failing to get along, end up dividing the land into multiple parcels. At times, that might become the only solution, but it is not what is best for the land. If it comes to that, the best thing for the land is to sell the land intact. It is a lot easier to divide money than it is to divide land.

Scenic Farm barn by Simms Brooks

A good place to start is to get the farm into a suitable form of ownership such as a limited liability corporation and have a well thought out management agreement. This at least gives those that follow a workable roadmap.

Our family has been blessed to have managed our Farm with virtually no disagreement. This is made easier in that the three owners in my generation (Charlie, Betsy and myself) have always viewed the land through the same lens, and that being attempting to manage it in a way that our parents would have done it. This has not been difficult since we have always looked at the land more or less the way that they did. The result of 75 years of similar management has resulted in a very timeless environment.

Hayfield by David Hartfield

Some years ago the Farm was organized as an LLC and implemented a well thought out management plan. This structure will become more important in the future as subsequent generations assume responsibility for management. The likelihood of everyone agreeing on how the Farm will be run in the future will certainly get harder for subsequent generations as the number of owners increases. Our management agreement takes a simple approach. It requires that each of the three families be represented by a single manager and each family has one vote with the majority ruling.

It provides a formula for buying out a minority owner in such a way that favors the remaining owners without being unfair to the exiting member. It should be pointed out that none of these heirs had to personally buy any of this land, and that usually minority partners have no good exit strategy should they desire to get out.

Scenic Farm road by Simms Brooks

I think that the thing that makes me the most comfortable and confident about the future is the fact that we have a conservation easement on our land. I have already said that our easement has been in place for almost 20 years now, and I don't think that I have ever heard a single word of regret voiced by a family member in that time. I believe that the thing about the easement that gives me the most peace of mind is the fact that at some point in the future, the family discovers that they can't get along about over how to manage the Farm, or find that the can't afford to keep it up and manage it properly, they can sell it, subject to the terms of the conservation easement of course. In this event, all would know that it would continue to be managed the way we said it would according to the terms of the easement no matter who owns it. This would be true in perpetuity. That fact gives me a real sense of peace.

Random Thoughts

While working on this book, I had many thoughts and memories that flashed through my mind that I did not think warranted a complete chapter by themself, but worth mentioning somewhere. I started writing them down as they came up and ended up coming up with a pretty good list creating the genesis of this chapter which we will call Random Thoughts.

Some years ago, we were having quite a problem with coyotes around our house, so I hired a trapper to try to eliminate some of them. After several days, he reported in that he had caught several possums and racoons and three bobcats and no coyotes. I said, "Jim, I hope that you did not kill the bobcats." He looked at me like I had lost my mind and said, "Boss, I would like you to tell me how you would get a 30 pound bobcat out of a leg-hold trap!" I said, "I guess you have a pretty good point" and said no more about it.

Nilla (my mother) gave me much wonderful advice as I was growing up. I think that the most useful life lesson that she ever told me was when I was preparing to leave for Vermont in 1964. She said, "There are three things that you should never, EVER, discuss in public. They are politics, religion, and money!" I found that to be very useful advice when I got to Vermont, and also later as I went through the army, and later as a businessman encountering all types of people from all over the country and the world. The takeaway is that if you can remove those three things from a conversation, I have found that everyone is pretty much the same. I find this advice especially useful today as I watch friends lose friends over what they are willing to say either publicly or on social media.

My parents both taught me to love the land and do the best that you can with what you have.

When I was no more than five or six, I was walking with Nilla and her beautiful friend, Anna King, up into one of the lovely coves above the road into the Farm House. Suddenly, we stated smelling smoke, and as we rounded the next bend, we came upon a working whiskey still. The two men operating it quickly disappeared, and the three of us quickly beat tracks back to the house, whereupon Nilla informed Charlie (my father) about the incident. Other than being told to stay away from that area, I didn't hear any more about it for a while, until several months later Nilla and Anna took me back to the site and showed me that the still had been destroyed. Stills were still fairly commonplace in the early 1950s, and one of the jobs of the local sheriff was to bust them up when he found one. My guess is that Charlie took Tom Rye, our local sheriff's deputy, to the site, and had him destroy it. See picture above.

Destroyed still at Farm

Charlie's idea of taking me fishing as a young boy was having me paddle him while he fished. Two good things happened from this experience besides him catching most of the fish. First, I became an expert paddler, and second, I learned how to fish from the back of the boat. To this day, I prefer to be the primary paddler, and I prefer to fish from the back. This method works best because I am almost always the better paddler and can keep the boat in the best position for us both to catch more fish. I have often wondered whether that was Charlie's intended strategy, or whether he was simply looking for someone to paddle him.

For as long as I knew him, Charlie always carried the

same pocketknife. Oh, it wasn't the "same" knife, because he lost them regularly. But it was the same knife, a small, thin, bone handled Shrade folding pocketknife. Robert always carried one just like it, that I am sure Charlie kept him supplied in. About 20 years after Charlie's death, one of the grandchildren found the knife shown below in the swimming hole in the pond at the Farm House. Having been under water for at least 20 years, the blades had rusted away, but it was instantly recognizable as my father's knife. Just seeing it stirred many poignant memories.

Charlie's knife after spending 20 years under water

One beautiful late spring Sunday morning, I was riding my horse, Sir, accompanied by my faithful Labrador, Amos on the part of the Farm known as the East Side. We passed close by a pile of brush covered with scuppernong vines, and a wild turkey hen with a broken wing scurried out of the tangle and ran down the road dragging her injured wing. Before I could stop him, Amos took off after her at top speed. She lead him on this chase for about 100 yards. About the time that I was figuring out that the hen didn't have a broken wing at all, and that it was all a ruse to get Amos away from her young, she turned on him and started chasing him, flapping her wings and making quite a ruckus. Amos tucked his tail between his legs and started running back to me with the hen right behind him. Somehow I kept my wits enough to quickly dismount just as Amos ran under Sir for shelter from this "hell-bitch". The hen stopped about 10 feet away, still making quite a ruckus. When she decided that we were sufficiently intimidated, she turned and started strutting up the road away from us, clucking as she went, and I am sure she was signaling her babies to follow her, now that the threat was eliminated!

Another similar event with different characters occurred one summer evening when Betsy, Nilla, and I were sitting on

Horse pasture in the evening

our front porch with our dogs and sharing a glass of wine. We frequently see deer that time of day moving from the woods on one side of the horse pasture to the corn field on the other side or vice versa. Well that evening, a doe appeared with two small fawns, moving from right to left across the pasture. They were pretty quickly spotted by the dogs, and they immediately gave chase. The deer took off for the tree line. The Jack Russells gave up about halfway across the field, but Nilla's dog, Max, a golden retriever cross, was not to be deterred. The doe cleared the fence easily and one of the fawns squeezed through underneath. The second fawn could not figure out the way through, and as Max closed on it, the enraged doe jumped back over the fence and landed almost on top of Max. Going on the attack, she ran at Max while flashing her sharp hooves at him. Max, caught completely off guard, yielded quickly and turned tail back to the house running as fast he could. It wasn't over however, and the doe chased him all the way back across the field where he sought shelter with Nilla on the porch. The doe stopped at the fence in front of the house and stood, stomping her feet and snorting for about 30 seconds, and then turned and confidently trotted across the field, back to her babies, another threat eliminated! Never underestimate the power and will of a mother protecting her young. They are aggressive and totally fearless!

Growing up, we usually kept four to six beehives on our Farm and did so up until the mid-1980s. Many memories are associated with the bees, some good, some not so good. Gathering the honey was a family event, with all available hands on deck to help with the harvest. It was usually on a very hot, sunny day when a high percentage of workers were away from the hive, hence less mad bees to deal with. Charlie would smoke the hive which would kind of sedate the bees for a while, and we would begin to remove the combs holding the honey and take it to a safe place where another crew could remove the honey from the combs. Sooner or later the bees would figure what was happening and get mad, real mad! That complicated the process a great deal. You could hear the pitch of their wings change when they were angry, and every now and then, a bee would find its way into your suit or head net. Charlie had a high threshold of pain and bee stings didn't seem to bother him a whole lot. I can't say the same for me, and I can tell you, two or three bees inside your suit would quickly take the fun out of the whole exercise. Nilla and Charlie really enjoyed putting up the honey and took a lot of pride in giving it as Christmas presents. The bee project ended tragically for the bees themselves. We had moved the hives from near the Farm House over to near the hay field behind where Betsy and I live in the early 80s. After a couple of years, we had a serious problem with fall army worms in the hayfield. Without even thinking about the bees at all, we sprayed the field with a powerful pesticide, and in doing so, killed all the bees. I convinced my father not to replace them. He was too old to be the beekeeper at that time, and I simply didn't have the time.

By the time that I was a teenager we were starting to see quite a few deer around the Farm. We were still trying to figure out how to hunt them, so on most hunts we didn't get anything, but occasionally someone would get lucky and would kill one. This created great excitement for everyone on the hunt, whether just a couple of hunters or more than a dozen, and the aftermath was often more fun than the hunt itself. There were several ancient rituals in play, such as the cutting of shirttails for a missed deer, or the bloodying of the face for a hunter's first kill. There was lots of storytelling and a certain amount of beer drunk and as much as anything, the old-fashioned deer hunt

Long ago deer hunt circa 1970

was a social event. When it came time to clean and butcher the deer people pitched in and made light work of it. Then came the disposal of the remains and what to do with them. Well in those days, we always had some pigs penned up, and Robert taught me the trick to simply dump the remains into the pig pen. Come back the next day and they would be gone, and I mean gone! No skin, no hair, no guts, no eyeballs, no antlers. Gone!

Many things have changed with wildlife over the years that I am no longer surprised at what happens in nature on the Farm. we have always had some alligators in the

Treye with 12 foot 2 inch Alligator legally removed from our pond 2015

156

neighborhood but now we have so many and some are very large.

One of the many crops Charlie experimented with at the Farm in the early years was sugar cane and then making his own cane syrup at a conveniently located neighborhood syrup mill. The mill was located on a piece of land that is now part of the Farm in an area known as Romans Bottom. The mill was powered by a mule attached to a long shaft and continuously walking the shaft in a circle providing the horsepower to grind the molasses from the cane shoots and into a vat to be made into the syrup. Our cane was harvested by hand and hauled in a wagon to the mill. I remember going to the mill as a very young boy with Nilla and Charlie and watching the process. Nothing remains of the syrup mill and I can't identify the exact site, since I was so young when it was operating. It probably would be a good exercise to look for it with a metal detector. No telling what we would find.

It was always Charlie's idea for the Farm to be totally sustainable. Whenever possible, he used the resources on the Farm to provide as much of any needed material as he could. An example of this is that from the early years up into the early 80s, we made all of our own fence posts. Looking back on it, I'm not sure that it made a whole lot of sense, or that Charlie really saved any money by doing so. We did have an almost unlimited supply of six to ten inch pines. The young pines were cut into six and eight foot lengths and stacked in the woods where a tractor could reach them for later use. After they had dried for several months, Robert would send a group of his boys to the stack to scrape the bark off with straightened out hoes. The posts were then hauled in a wagon back to the farmstead where they were loaded six to eight at a time into a large horizontal vat that contained a mixture of pentachlorophenol and diesel fuel, where the dried out posts would soak up the chemicals to cure them. After several days in the vat, the posts were removed and stacked to dry. This process made a very good fence post. We still have some in the ground that have been there for over 60 years. It was very labor intensive, however. In those days, Robert always had a group of growing boys that needed to be kept busy and to earn a little extra money either for themselves or for Robert. After Robert retired, and Johnny Johnson was the Farm Manager, we simply no longer had the available labor supply to make this process viable. About the time that we were figuring out that we could buy fence posts cheaper than we could make them, pentachlorophenol started getting some very negative press about how environmentally dangerous it was. That was the end of the fence post enterprise!

50-year-old fence made with fence posts produced on the farm

As previously mentioned, we use a fairly intensive prescribed fire regimen in our woodlands on the Farm and have concluded that it is a very cost-effective way to manage them. It is fast, inexpensive, and not hard if you know what you are doing and plan your burn carefully. Two rules that I have adopted over the years are that if you don't end up with a few singed-up tops, you probably aren't burning hot enough, and if you don't get scared enough to get some adrenaline moving at least once, then you probably are not burning hot enough!

I love to manage the land for ducks, deer and turkeys, and spend as much time doing it as I ever did but find that I spend less time hunting them each year. I have all but stopped hunting turkeys all together. I don't really know why that is. I love to see them, but I just don't have much interest in shooting one, and I guess that I would rather have one of the grandchildren get one. I also guess that it is not as much fun getting up early in the mornings as it used to be.

Several years ago, our daughter, Elizabeth Cate Grove, closed down her training barn, which is back towards Columbia a few miles, and accepted a position as a high school counselor in Columbia. She still

Elizabeth with some of her riding students

loves to ride and maintains a few clients, who she instructs at the Farm when she finds the time. Its great having the increased horse activity again and having the young people around. It is even greater having Elizabeth here regularly, and she is a big help to us in our daily barn maintenance.

I have always thought that managing a piece of land is akin to making a work of art on a grand scale. The decisions that you make will likely change the way an area looks for the next 50 to 100 years. Collectively, these decisions create a certain flavor for a farm or woodland. You leave your mark! I see the marks left by Nilla and Charlie, or Robert, or Johnny, or Treye, and I know who made them and when. Or, it could be a mark made by me, all part of the tapestry. A 100 years from now, people will still see these marks. They might not know who made them, but they will know somebody did.

Our wonderful Jack Russell terrier, Dottie, died last weekend unexpectantly before sending this manuscript off to the publisher. It was a gut-wrenching experience. She became very ill the weekend before after going totally blind overnight. We watched her deteriorate as the week wore on before deciding that we had to let her go. On her last night on earth, I sat on our porch holding her in my lap, knowing that it was our last chance to do this together. I just sat there stroking her, rubbing the silky hair inside of her ears, savoring the smell of her hair, just not wanting to stop, afraid that I might forget what she felt like and what she smelled like. I realize as I write this that it was not her that was suffering. It was us. She was the ultimate dog. She had a wonderful life and was loved by so many people. I have never known a dog that had so many friends that will truly miss her.

It has been amazing for us to live basically our whole lives on this timeless Farm. Every day I see some reminder that triggers a poignant memory. It may be something that Nilla or Charlie planted or built reminds me of them. It may simply be a spot in the woods that reminds me of a good time or special event with a childhood friend in that spot that makes me think of them and the good times that we had together. Each day I ride in or out around Treye's house and it reminds me of the three families that have lived there over the course of my life, and it reminds me of what those three men have meant to the history of this Farm. I think maybe the most poignant time of all is when I take a late afternoon swim in the pond at the Farm House, and I can almost hear my parents sitting on the front porch, discussing the days events or what they might be doing the next day. This is something they did for as long as I knew them.

Acknowledgements

As with most books written by amateurs, they do not get completed without a lot of help from others. It has been very gratifying to find how responsive people have been after being asked for assistance in this project. When I first started writing *The Farm*, I knew I was quickly going to surpass my technological ability and was going to need help at every corner along the way.

All of my family, Betsy, Walker, Nilla, and Elizabeth, have been supportive and in editing and doing critiques on chapters as they came out. More importantly, they encouraged me to keep going. My granddaughter, Eliza, who is a junior at Clemson University was a lifesaver when it came time to get the chapters together and organized into a working manuscript and inserting the photographs. Speaking of photographs, that has become the most tedious part of this whole project. We had tons of old family photos to sort through, many just stuffed into boxes and some over 100 years old. Tedious as it was, it was also a lot of fun as I had forgotten that many of them even existed. The girls were a huge help with this phase. I did have access to some professional grade photography provided by a group of friends that specialize in wildlife and outdoor photography. Simms Brooks, Jim Kelly, Ron Ahle, Jane Willcox Salley, and David Hartfield were very generous in allowing me to use some of their spectacular images. Grover Rye was especially helpful in providing some old photos from Goodwill as was Larry Faulkenberry for allowing me to take some of my own. Stuart White, Executive Director of the Congaree Land Trust, has been supportive of this project from the beginning, and Mark Lowery, also with CLT, was very helpful in making map modifications for the COWASEE Basin and the Wateree River Corridor. Speaking of maps, Trip Chavis, Gordon Baker, and especially Bryson Lever with Milliken Forestry Company provided the necessary changes to the forestry mapping of the Farm to make them usable for the book. I especially want to thank my good friend John Cely for being willing to write the Foreword and to give this book some measure of credibility.

I sent rough manuscripts to eight friends, all published

writers or with experience in the publishing business, to seek editorial comment. They were, in no particular order, Wilmot Irvin, Warren Hughes (Pinky to me) who sent it on to Tom Poland, and John Snyder, John Cely, Hunter Smith, Frances Taylor and my niece, Sue Cate. I want to thank them all for taking the time to read my work and to offer back criticism, as well as words of encouragement. I came away feeling that I was on the right track. I must say that I felt strongly that I wanted my book to sound like me talking, so on occasion, I overruled their advice because their changes, while likely correct, did not sound like me. That is totally on me.

Diane Kennedy is a graphic designer who has provided invaluable help in preparing the manuscript into a suitable format to send to a publisher. She has also been very helpful by helping me think through the process as to how best to get it published. She designed the book and the cover. The front cover image was provided by Simms Brooks, and the rear cover photo was taken by John Cely on a memorable three day paddle down the Wateree River.

I contracted with BookBaby to help me publish and print this book. Isabel Imperatore with BookBaby has been very helpful throughout the process. She is very reachable, which is certainly important when you need to talk through an issue. She has helped to remove some of the mystery from this project for me.

Many thanks to the many friends and family members who read parts of the book and offered words of encouragement. Without that, I probably would have given up.

Lastly, I want to thank those many family and friends who helped to create the treasure trove of memories on this timeless Farm with me. Please know that I think of you each time I pass a spot where that memory occurred. Thank you.